Pratt Food Company

Pratt's Pointers on Cows, Sheep and Hogs

including their care, feeding, housing and diseases - containing valuable information from experienced authorities throughout the world

Pratt Food Company

Pratt's Pointers on Cows, Sheep and Hogs
including their care, feeding, housing and diseases - containing valuable information from experienced authorities throughout the world

ISBN/EAN: 9783337191191

Printed in Europe, USA, Canada, Australia, Japan

Cover: Foto ©Lupo / pixelio.de

More available books at **www.hansebooks.com**

Pratts Pointers

...ON...

COWS, SHEEP AND HOGS

INCLUDING

THEIR CARE, FEEDING, HOUSING AND DISEASES

CONTAINING

Valuable Information from Experienced Authorities Throughout the World.

PUBLISHED BY

PRATT FOOD COMPANY

Manufacturers of

PRATTS FOODS

The Greatest Animal and Poultry Regulators Known.

PHILADELPHIA, U. S. A.
CHICAGO, U. S. A.

PART I.

PRATTS POINTERS
ON
THE COW

CHAPTER I.

GENERAL SUGGESTIONS.

DAIRY FARMING In choosing a dairy farm, all necessary conditions for success in the business must be considered. It is an old saying that "the man makes the business," and this is particularly true of the dairyman. He must be patient and persevering, regular in methods of business, and neat in his habits. Level soil, well watered, makes the best farm land for dairy purposes, and if it is not naturally drained, artificial means should be used. The means of getting to and from a city should be looked after, and it is well to locate as near to a railroad as possible. If there is a natural spring on the premises the milk

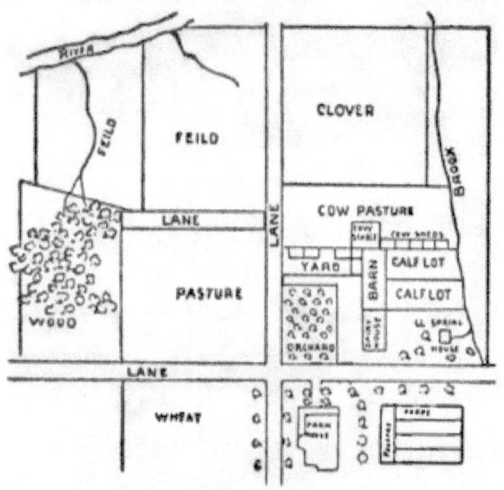

PLAN OF DAIRY FARM.

house should be placed either over, or very near it. In the illustration we show you how a dairy farm may be conveniently laid out.

STOCKING THE FARM — Next in importance is, of course, a careful and judicious selection of the stock. These are to be the dairyman's tools, and he will naturally want those from which he can derive the most benefit. Farmers who breed their own cows get superior milkers at moderate cost, if care is taken to raise only the calves of good milkers, and if the bull belongs to a family that gives milk of excellent quality and quantity.

| FORMING A HERD | The American cow is a descendant from many crossings, and in its veins is mixed blood impossible to name; nevertheless, |

it is the most reliable foundation upon which the dairy-

SHORT-HORN COW.

man can form a good herd. The "Short-horn," imported into America in the early part of this century, plainly shows in the native stock of the Middle States, while the blood of the "Devon" and "Ayrshire" shows in the breed down East. This may be accounted for by reason of the animals of this stock being better suited to thrive on the rough and poor pasture in that vicinity.

BREEDS OF COWS

The dairy farmer will naturally consider everything which contributes to the success of his undertaking, and a few words

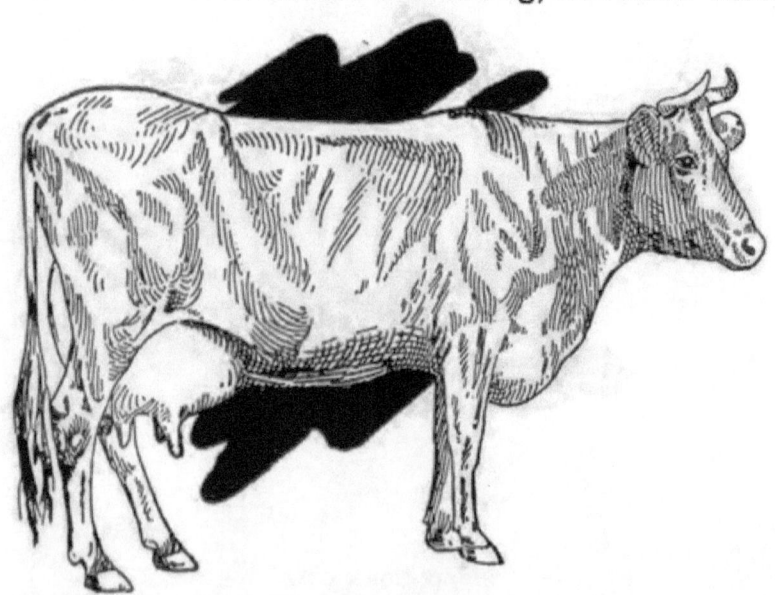

AYRSHIRE COW.

as to the different breed of cows might be of some value to him at this time. The Short-horn, probably the most valuable to the dairyman, is a native of the North of England and has been raised there for some time past. When no longer profitable as a milk producer, it fattens quickly and makes good beef.

Without underrating other breeds, the Ayrshire is often called "the model dairy cow," the milk being very rich in cream and easily turned into butter and cheese of choice quality.

From about the same part of the world come three of the best breeds of cows. The Jersey, Alderney and Guernsey. They differ from each other only in size and color, all of them being noted for the rich quality of their milk. The Jersey was at first more of an ornamental cow, but has since grown in favor with dairymen. It is a beautiful creature, light fawn color mixed with white, and with the gentlest expression in the large soft eyes. The horns are fine, black in color and gracefully curved, projecting over the forehead. (See illustration on back cover.)

Many farmers who have very rich and beautiful pasture land are fond of the Holstein breed which comes from the northern part of Holland. They are splendidly formed, and when no longer serviceable as milkers, they readily fatten and make excellent beef. (See illustration on front cover.)

Holland also furnishes another breed, but one that is more popular. It is black with a broad belt of white entirely around the body, and hence it derives its name of Belted or Blanketed. They have been carefully bred and have gained a high reputation for milk and butter.

The Swiss have become famous in connection with their dairy products, and quite naturally. Their cows are excellent producers of milk and butter. They are very domestic, docile and gentle, and a number of them imported into New England some years ago show that they are fitted for the climate of this country. They are now to be found in many other localities and are greatly valued.

The Devon is the oldest race of cattle in existence, and year after year produces the same type. In color it is a rich dark red without other mixture. They are good dairy cows, the yield of milk and flavor of butter being unsurpassed. Devon beef is superior to any other ; is tender, sweet and with just enough fat to make it delicious.

England furnishes a cow very much like the Devon, it being also red in color, but it is without horns, and this is considered a very desirable feature in dairy cattle. Their milk and quality of beef is excellent.

HORNLESS COWS
In this connection it might be well to say a word about this animal, as many persons hold different opinions. Horns prove dangerous weapons, and many accidents occur every year from the use of them by enraged animals. To avoid the possibility of this, the question of dishorning calves when very young has been much agitated and to certain degree put in practice, sufficiently to prove that it can be done easily and without pain. These calves afterwards bred together will soon produce hornless stock, which in time will inherit polled heads without further effort. Although all these breeds have been mentioned for the benefit of dairymen, they as a rule give preference to the Holstein, Ayrshire, Jersey and Guernsey.

CHAPTER II.

FOOD FOR THE COWS.

THE DAIRY COW
If you expect a liberal product of milk, butter and cheese, quite naturally the cow must be given the food that is most suitable for this purpose. No matter how excellent her milking qualities, she cannot make up deficiencies arising from improper feeding. How to derive the most profit from the smallest outlay is the most important

question with the dairyman, as it is with any other man in business. He should first supply the natural wants of the animal, and as much additional material as she can convert into milk and cream. Milk has the same composition as the animal, and contains every element to support her. Therefore, to feed the dairy cow to insure successful results, the farmer must exercise great care. Pratts Food will sustain bodily health and strength by regulating the bowels, blood and digestive organs ; it produces more milk and of a very rich quality. Many experienced farmers have long since acquainted themselves with the important value of its use, and in consequence it is universally used by thousands of dairymen throughout the United States and many foreign countries.

PROFITABLE CROPS Dairy stock must be fed properly, and to do this requires close study. Grass is the first and most important crop, as it is depended upon for summer pasture, and the meadows also supply hay for winter feeding. Timothy, red-top, and red clover are the varieties most used by American farmers. Hay, if properly cut in the first stages of blossoming, will keep all the sweetness and good qualities of fresh grass. Fodder-corn ranks next to grass, either when fed green or dried for winter use. Clover is third in value, and profitable, because if managed properly will grow for several years with one planting. Carrots, beets and parsnips are important as a root-crop for winter feeding. The wise farmer will grow his own fodder.

VARIETY OF FOOD

Oats, ground, are an expensive food, but if purchased at fairly reasonable prices, are profitable on account of the manure element they contain. Oats have, however, been largely rejected from the list of dairy goods, as it has been proved that the butter is light in color and inferior in quality.

In America the usual and most-used food on the dairy farm is corn, but it gives the best results when fed in proper proportions with other foods. Unless given too freely, it never affects injuriously the milk glands, but it has been demonstrated that it is used with the most favorable influence when given in the form of fine bolted yellow meal. Hominy chops, wheat bran and husks of grain generally, while valuable for the nitrogen they contain and their profitable returns in manure, are so indigestible as to require great care in their use.

Peas are milk-producing if used as food in connection with corn meal and pasture. Furthermore, they are not only nutritious in themselves, but are an aid to digestion. Rice meal is a rich food, and most satisfactory results are obtained by feeding it.

BREWERS' GRAINS Much has been said and written about this kind of food as being very objectionable for dairy cattle, and, therefore, bitterly protested against. This is only true when used after fermentation has taken place, as it then influences the milk, giving it an unpleasant taste, which is also noticeable in the butter. When fresh and sweet, brewers' grains are a clean, wholesome food, producing milk in good quality and quantity.

TEST FOR THE DIGESTIBILITY OF FOODS The digestibility of food measures its value, and this the intelligent farmer ascertains by certain reliable tests which he can use every bit as well as a scientist. First, as to the cream. Cream gauges set in a frame and the name of the cow written on a tablet just above each one, easily determines the richness of the milk. Once each week they are filled with the milk of the separate cows, and the amount of cream that rises, accurately decides the profit of one kind of feed over another. A butter test is also made by the use of the smallest-sized churn, the butter afterwards weighed and compared with quantity of milk given, and also, the record of the cream gauge of the especial cow. This determines without question the best food for the least cost, and hence the dairyman may know beforehand what rate of profit to expect from his labor and outlay. The dairy farm thus managed is not a business of chance, but of comparative certainty, as milk and butter are counted among life's necessities and always with good market value. The milk may be tested in this manner: A spring balance, commonly known as a weighing-hook, is put up in the cow stable, and upon this the pail is hung and the milk of each cow weighed separately.

The weight is taken to the half-pound, which is near enough to be of practical service. This weight, after deducting the weight of the pail, is marked down on paper, and a careful count kept from week to week. This habit, if maintained, is a guide to show value of different foods, and also to show when anything is amiss with a particular cow. It is remarkable how uniform the weight of milk from the same animal is, time after time, when regularly fed and managed. It may be well to mention that Pratts Food **creates perfect digestion, and pays largely when fed constantly.**

SALT | Farmers should consider the necessity of salt for the dairy cow, to make up that thrown off in the daily waste of the system. Chemistry teaches that an ounce and a half should be given every twenty-four hours in regular rations, mixed with each feed. While this is required for the animal's health and comfort, an excess of salt is bad. The barrel should never be left uncovered where it can be eaten in quantity.

CHAPTER III.

WATER SUPPLY, CATTLE SHEDS, ETC.

SPRINGS, WELLS AND CISTERNS | If a spring is not available, probably the safest water supply is a well, placed at a distance from the barnyard or stable. It should be furnished with a pump, and surrounded by a neat platform, and everything about it kept clean and free from impurities. Pure water is always needed in the dairy business, and to secure this should be a chief point when purchasing a farm for that purpose. It is most desirable to have a stream of water running through the pasture, and coming from a cold and permanent spring. If possible, it is best to own the source of the stream, so that it may be controlled and the water kept pure; otherwise it will injure the health of the stock, or impart a bad taste to the milk.

If neither a spring or small creek be on the premises, a very good substitute is a well-constructed rain-water cistern, an excellent form of which is here given. A

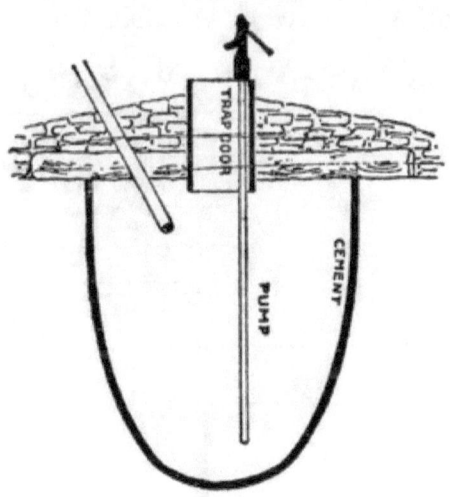

WATER CISTERN.

force pump is the most convenient attachment to a cistern, as by means of a hose-pipe water can be sent wherever needed, in any part of the yard or stable. A large amount of water is used in cleaning the pans, pails and other utensils required for the care of milk and butter-making. For this purpose a spring or well, either in or very near the milk house, will save time and labor and can be easily secured.

DAIRY BUILDINGS | The different buildings in connection with the dairy farm must be constructed with a view of deriving the greatest convenience in carrying on the business and for the best care and comfort of the cows. Neatness, economy of

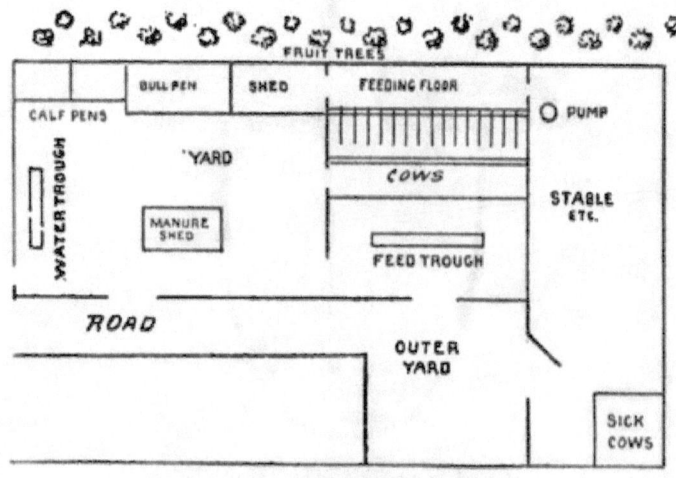

STABLE, PEN AND YARD.

room, and opportunity to pass readily from one building to another, are points important to consider when building. We show you here a plan which invites these advantages in an admirable manner.

STABLE FLOORS

A suitable floor is essential, and if the stable is without a cellar underneath an earth floor is better than any other. If of good clay or gravel it will harden and become perfectly solid and need no repairs. If the stable has a manure cellar under the entire building, the cellar floor

PLANK FLOOR.

should be of cement and the stable floor made of double plank. This should be laid with a gutter, emptied by trap doors, and the floor frequently scrubbed and given a coat of whitewash, to keep it sweet and clean. We here show you a good plank floor of this sort.

YARD, COW STABLE AND SHED

The yard should be large enough to give ample room for milking sheds, water troughs, fodder racks and pens. Half an acre affords comfortable accommodation for thirty cows. No other animals should be permitted within the enclosure. The cow shed grows in favor with the dairyman, as it offers equal protection and comfort to animals, without the danger from fire and smoke suffocation attending the ordinary closed stable where hay is stored. Humanity is always on the lookout to make improvements for the care of dumb animals. In the

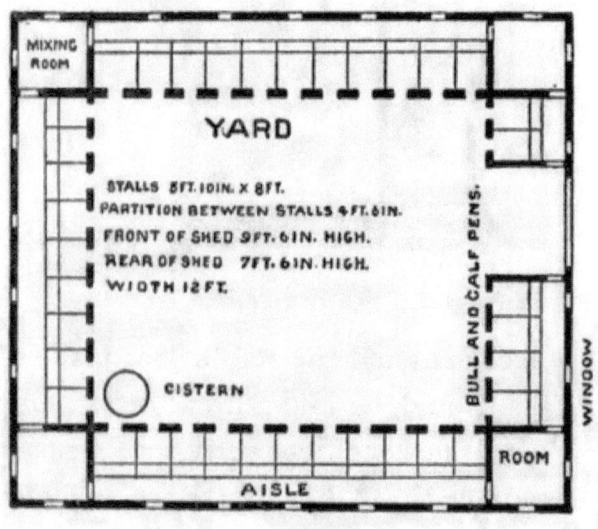

COW SHED.

modern cow shed, cows are left loose in the stalls, except on occasions when they are fastened by rings screwed in the sides at convenient height. These stalls have a double door, the upper part left open when ventilation is necessary, and each has its individual feed trough.

FAMILY COW

Fresh pure milk, and plenty of cream, add greatly to good living, and are now counted among the luxuries of the table. To enjoy them at their best, experience teaches that it

HORSE AND COW STABLE AND POULTRY SHED.

is necessary to keep a cow, unless very fortunately situated in reference to milk supply. The stable can be comfortably located near a dwelling and yet not prove

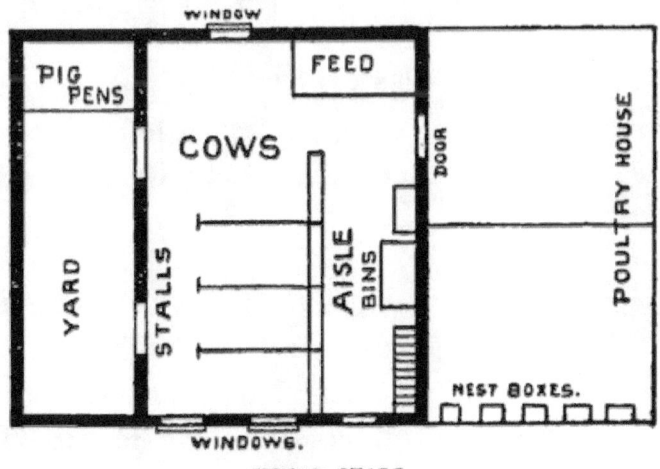

CHEAP STALL.

objectionable to the most particular housewife. The building can be ornamental and, to economize room, devoted to several purposes, a wood shed, garden tool closet, and even a milk room ; all under the same roof. A plan here given has a poultry annex and accommodates two horses in addition to the cow stable.

A very cheap stable in connection with a summer home affords comfort and convenience at astonishingly small outlay, and can easily be constructed.

In the West and South, where timber is abundant and cheap, the open cow shed is often seen. It has a

OPEN COW SHED.

tight roof with closed ends, forming a loft to store hay in, and affords shelter for feeding and milking in stormy weather.

CLEANLINESS ABOUT THE STABLE | Milk is an absorbent, and unless the stable is kept free from bad odors, they will destroy the natural taste and sweetness of the milk and give an unpleasant flavor to the butter.

If the air of a stable is impure, the offensive matter is taken into the blood of the cow, and in this way poisons the source of the milk. To test this, strew the stable floor with onions, turnips, leeks or other strong-smelling vegetable growth, and it will very soon be detected in the milk. It is equally true that a green lawn and flowers with sweet scent around the stable will improve the flavor of milk and butter. This forms a picturesque feature of many English dairies, whose stalls are placed among grass and thickets of roses. The stable should be well aired and ventilated daily. A neat covering of leaves and cut straw on the floor, the gutter filled with fresh earth and freely dusted over with plaster. The use of a solution of copperas, mixed in a barrel of water, sprinkled freely from a watering-pot over the floor each morning after it has been swept, will sweeten the air and afford relief from flies. Afterward, the floor should be sprinkled with sand to prevent the cows from slipping while it is damp. If the stable windows be covered in summer with wire gauze to protect the animals from mosquitoes and troublesome insects in general, it will greatly add to the milk supply. Green slat blinds used to darken the windows will not interfere with proper ventilation if turned half-way open, and will also add to the advantage of the milk supply.

BAD EFFECTS OF IMPURE AIR

Impure air affects the health of animals as it does of persons, and it will be observed that sickness is much more frequent where it exists. This proves that the dairyman cannot be too particular in his surroundings, if he is to be successful. Perfect cleanliness must be observed in the smallest detail, not occasionally, but constantly and always.

COMFORTABLE COWS ARE PROFITABLE

Cows should be made comfortable, for if fretted and worried they yield less milk. A wide and easy door should be provided for them to pass in and out of the stable, and everything that tends to annoy them should be guarded against with extreme care. Kindness is all-important, and to kick, strike or yell at an animal is against the dairyman's interest, and it will in every instance lessen the flow of milk. A prominent dairyman was asked "how cows should be treated." His reply was forcible, by way of a lesson: "Cows should be treated with gentleness and with consideration for their comfort and your own profit." To obtain pure, sweet milk and choicest butter and cheese the cows must be thoroughly brushed and currycombed each day. They should be fastened at such a distance from each other that they cannot hook or crowd, and yet it is not wise to waste space. Cows should be stalled every night throughout the year—in winter for warmth and in summer to keep them cool and protected from flies and mosquitoes.

DAILY DUTIES — In summer the cows should be milked at five o'clock in the morning, then well watered and taken to pasture. They should be brought home between five and six o'clock in the evening, milked, watered, given a measure of Pratts Food and comfortably stabled for the night. In winter it is best to keep cows in the stable until midday and then turn them into the yard for fresh air and exercise until time for the evening milking. Never stint cows in food, as it is always best to give them all they will eat. It is unnecessary to state that striking matches, smoking, using kerosene lamps or candles should be forbidden in the stable. Lanterns, filled with the safest oil, should be hung high out of reach of accident in doing the necessary work at night. These points, small in themselves, are really the corner-stone of the dairyman's success, and only a fair trial will convince of their importance.

CHAPTER IV.

RAISING STOCK.

BUTTER VALUE OF COWS

As has been previously said, cows are the dairyman's instruments, and upon their excellence his success depends, and must be chosen for the amount and quality of their milk. If an animal yields only milk enough each day to produce one pound of butter, she is not worth as much as the cow that produces two pounds. A little thought will show that in the one case you care for and feed one cow to obtain two pounds of butter, while in the other you feed and care for two cows and get the same result.

COST OF SUCCESSFUL BREEDING

The practical dairyman understands the value of his stock, and wishes to increase rather than lessen it. As to breeding, a few simple facts may be given, which can be easily understood. Different traits and qualities are transmitted to each generation. Breeders of fancy and pure breed stock claim that fancy stock only have this power of transmitting characteristics, and use this argument to maintain the high price of their cattle. This is not so, however, as all animals possess the same power, and whatever the breed, if the dairyman selects the best cows and mates them with a bull of pure breed, and continues this course with the calves, he will find the result very satisfactory. The milking quality is the sole point the dairyman need consider; he will experience loss if he attempts to compete with professionals in stock raising for market. The wise farmer will rear his own herd, and make it superior and valuable enough to repay him for all his care and trouble. If for any reason he sells any of his cattle, he will always sell the poor, and not the good ones.

BREED DEPENDS MUCH UPON FEED — Feeding and training improves and increases the value of all animals, and none more so than dairy stock. The purer the breed, the more careful must be the treatment to keep it up to the standard. Inferior food and indifferent care, too often given to common stock, will very soon retrograde the finest pure breed. Pratts Food, properly used, will do more to improve the breed than anything known; it makes healthy and contented cows, which in itself is the greatest known advantage in improving dairy cows.

CHOICE OF BREED — The most useful dairy cow should be known at a glance by a thorough dairyman. He should know how important it is to select a good breed, and must not confine his choice to any particular one. The Short-horn or Holstein prove the most satisfactory in the production of milk and cream. For butter the Jersey and Ayrshire are the prime favorites. Dairymen usually prefer to purchase the bull when yet a calf, but to do this successfully the pedigree should be known of the dam, and both the grand-dams should be inquired of in order to be certain that they were of the best milking quality.

BREEDING PERIODS OF THE COW When the cow is about a year old, or at the latest, fourteen months, she commences to have what are called breeding periods. These occur about every twenty or twenty-one days. A cow carries her calf nine months, although this varies in exceptional cases, and is sometimes less and sometimes a longer period. In many instances it has been found that the male calf is carried for several days longer than the female. Jersey cows differ slightly in this respect, and have been frequently known to breed some months earlier than other breeds.

FEEDING THE COW The cow with a calf has a new demand upon her system, and this must be met by proper feeding. Pratts Food at this time is especially valuable. Her feed should be liberal and of nutritious quality, but overfeeding is a mistake to be avoided. A calf partakes of the mother's life and disposition, and if she has any especial fault or tendency, this should, if possible, be prevented in the calf. The surest way to accomplish this is by liberal feeding and extreme kindness and tender care of the cow at this critical period. In this manner a calf can be easily made to inherit desirable traits, which in time will become natural and a marked characteristic.

THE BULL | The bull should not be put to too much use. This is especially so of a young bull. The second year he can generally be put to twice as much work as the first. It is better to charge more for outside service and admit only a few cows than to take a smaller price and be compelled to admit more. The owner of the cow will take better care of the calf he has to pay more for. A pen and yard adjoining the cow stable and barnyard should be provided for the bull, and when he is needed the cow should be led into this yard and securely fastened in one corner. The bull is then let out of the stall until he has accomplished his service. The cow is taken to a separate pen where a loose stall is provided for her, and afterwards she may be returned to the stable. The feeding of Pratts Food to bulls is more than repaid by the insurance of effective service and good health.

THE BULL A DANGEROUS ANIMAL — The dairyman should remember that a bull is always dangerous and never to be trusted. Although not to be treated cruelly, he must be kept in subjection, and at the first sign of disobedience conquered with a rawhide. A sight of this instrument of torture will soon become associated with remembrance of pain, and its use will be seldom required. The animal should never be petted or given the least freedom, however fine he may be or great the pride of his owner in his beauty or expense. Every year valuable lives are sacrificed from this foolish trifling with favorite bulls which are believed to be docile and under perfect control.

REMOVING THE CALF FROM THE MOTHER — The most intelligent dairymen now decide that the calf should be taken away from its mother almost as soon as it is born. This makes the cow, within a few days, useful in the dairy and with abundant milk product that can be turned to profit in butter. The calf becomes fond of its keeper and exceedingly domestic and gentle, which are excellent traits for its future as a dairy cow. The cow is kept in a roomy box stall and well cared for until able to join the herd again.

RAISING THE CALF | The calf should be placed in a clean, dry pen (see illustration) and given the entire milk, warm from its mother, twice each day for four days, while from the first, Pratts Food should be fed to the calf in small doses. After that it can be given half skimmed and half fresh milk, as

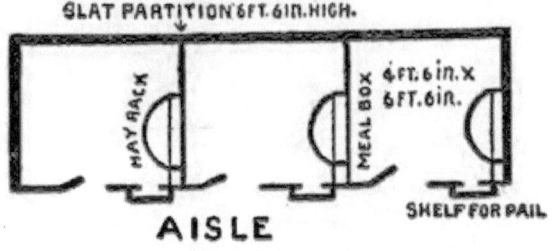

PEN FOR CALVES.

cream and fat are not necessary for its early growth. A good frame of bones and healthy muscles can be supplied quite as well if the skimmed milk is given at a temperature of eighty degrees. Three quarts in the morning and three quarts in the evening are sufficient at first; but this amount must be gradually increased until at six months old it will consume (in addition to other food) six quarts at each feeding. In winter, after the first month, it may be given a little sweet early clover hay, and in the summer a small lot can be enclosed by a portable fence that can be moved to any suitable spot, where it can exercise its limbs and eat the fresh grass. When six or eight months old the young heifer takes her place in the cow stable, and is liberally fed with regular rations. She is growing, and needs food to aid her in the process; and even if she fattens, no harm will come from it, if she grows large and strong in proportion. The first lesson the little calf should be taught is affection for its keeper, and this can be done by petting and kindness. By this method of raising the calf, the mother forgets her young, and to both cow and calf it becomes the only way, and finally, like other habits, hereditary with the race.

A MODEL CALF PEN — The calf should be tied from the first, by a little leather strap around its neck, with a ring attached, to which a small rope is fastened by a snap hook, and this is attached to a larger ring in the side of the pen. On one side of the calf pen is a rack for hay, and outside, in front, a shelf where the pail is put with the milk. A slide door will allow the calf to put its head through and drink, although so arranged that it cannot overturn the pail. Calves are very stupid, and while they cannot be trained by beating and force, they learn much from patience and gentleness.

CHAPTER V.

MILK AND CREAM.

FOUR RULES TO BE OBSERVED
The proper care of milk and cream for butter-making can be stated in four rules. First, the milk should be set in a perfectly pure atmosphere and surroundings. Second, with a moderate circulation of moist air. Third, the temperature should not exceed sixty degrees in summer, or fall below forty degrees in winter. Fourth, perfectly clean utensils, and not too much light, which, it is said, will take from the butter the deep, rich color that distinguishes the best quality.

STRAINING THE MILK
The milk should be strained with great care to prevent any speck of dust or chance hair remaining in the fluid. The milk should first pass through the fine lip-strainer of the pail, and afterwards through two fine wire gauze strainers. People are more particular about milk and butter

than any other articles of food, and more easily disgusted if anything is discovered amiss with them, either in flavor or cleanliness. For this reason, many makers of choice, high-priced butter insist upon the extra precaution of straining the milk a third and last time through fine double muslin. While this is troublesome and requires time, and is often regarded as catering too much to unnecessary fancies of customers, it nevertheless pays in reputation and profit to the dairyman in the end.

VALUE OF TESTS The elements contained in cow's milk are sugar, caseine, salts, fat and water. Fat, which is the cream, varies in amount in the milk of different cows. This proves the value of tests, which will decide for the dairyman whether he has inferior cows in his herd, and if so, which they are, that he may dispose of them before he suffers loss of time and profit. Weighing the milk, examining the cream gauge and churning the cream of each cow separately will settle this important question without a doubt. The largest milker is by no means certain to be the producer of the most butter; therefore, to decide the quality of the milk is even more necessary than its quantity.

METHODS OF SEPARATING

Cream, being the fatty part of milk, will rise to the top more or less rapidly, according to the temperature and the manner in which it is set. There are three methods of separating the cream from the milk, and each farmer must decide which is best and most suited to the convenience of his especial dairy. The deep pail system, used in Sweden and known as the "Schwartz method," has been a valuable assistance in butter-making of late years. The advantage claimed for this is that in the twenty inch deep pails, set in ice water at a temperature of forty-five degrees, the cream will rise in twelve hours, while the milk will remain sweet for seventy-two hours. The shallow pan system is almost universal in private farm dairies, and quite as good, without the expense of tank, ice, etc., which necessarily add much to the labor also. The airy, dry cellar or milk house with thick walls furnishes every facility for raising the cream in the simple old way, which, after all, seems easiest.

The third method promises to work a revolution in dairy practice everywhere, and is already accepted by most creamers throughout the country. "The Centrifugal Creamer" is the remarkable invention of a Swede. It has been awarded medals by different societies of agriculture whenever exhibited. The inventor claims that the cream can be separated entirely from the milk as soon as it is drawn from the cow and sufficiently cooled; that the quantity of butter is largely increased thereby, and the labor astonishingly reduced, because, as the milk is not set, the lifting and cleansing of pails, pans, etc., is done away with; that the skimmed milk is perfectly sweet, and therefore can be used or sold for any desired purpose. The cream is

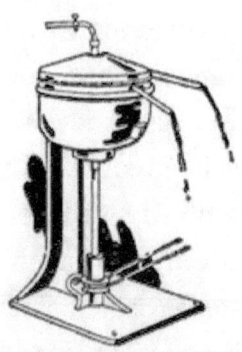

CENTRIFUGAL CREAMER.

put in bulk to ripen or sour just to the point fit for churning, and as it is separated in a perfectly pure condition, the flavor of the butter is said to be superior. This machine, when first brought into use, was very large and of two horse-power, but since then smaller ones have been made that can be worked by hand and suited to dairies where only twenty or thirty cows are kept. The dairyman who once sees it in operation regards this creamer as an excellent investment, and quickly avails himself of its many advantages.

| THE MILK CELLAR | Every house is supposed to be provided with a cellar, but most of them require very careful preparation before they are |

fit to receive milk. The milk cellar should be thoroughly

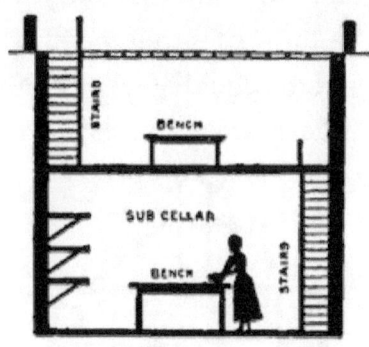

OUTSIDE MILK HOUSE.

cleansed, the walls treated to a heavy coat of whitewash, and a floor of smooth, hard cement laid. The windows must be protected by fine wire gauze, and every opportunity for free ventilation secured. The corners should have boxes filled with fresh lime, which must be frequently renewed to keep the cellar dry and sweet. Nothing by way of fruit or vegetables should be kept in a milk cellar, unless it is divided by a tight partition made from matched boards. An outside cellar, with sub-cellar, is possibly the best and most satisfactory plan for the shallow pan system, unless a regular milk house is erected.

THE MILK HOUSE | The most desirable milk house includes, not only a place to set the milk, but a room for skimming, churning and working the butter, and still another for packing and cold storage. It can be built of either wood, stone, or brick, and if well arranged, be equally serviceable in whichever material used. Where stone is used, everything can be

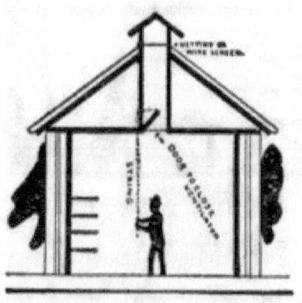

MILK HOUSE.

kept exquisitely clean by a constant flooding and washing down. A running stream of cold spring water is of great value in the milk house, and can be brought from a distance in an underground pipe. Its outlet should be over a tank, reservoir, or large sink furnished with a waste pipe to carry off the water when used.

MILKING

The cow is a nervous animal, easily frightened, and this state at once lessens both the quantity and quality of her milk. She must be milked gently and kindly, and with nothing to fret or disturb her during the process. If possible, the dairyman should divide his herd among the different milkers, so that the cow may be milked each time by the same person. Many farmers consider this a foolish whim, but good authority claims that in this way the animal becomes more docile and contented, and the milk product is larger. It is well known that cows are affectionate in their nature, and become attached to persons who milk them regularly and treat them kindly. Cows should be milked at intervals of twelve hours, as nearly as this can be conveniently managed, and either just before or after feeding; to milk while feeding is troublesome to both cow and milker. Constant watch must be kept that by some sudden movement of her foot the cow does not overturn the pail. If this happened accidentally, she should not be scolded or punished for it. When flies are troublesome in summer, a sheet spread over the animal is a protection, and will prevent the constant switching of her tail and kicking of her feet.

CHAPTER VI.

DAIRY UTENSILS.

The dairy business cannot be conducted successfully by chance or guesswork, neither can mistakes or accidents be overlooked. For every failure somebody is at fault, and the cost and labor of butter-making is entirely too great to take any risks on the result.

A dairyman should procure the best cows; those which have been well bred, fed and cared for, and in this way made comfortable and contented. After milking the cow and thoroughly straining the milk in the cleanest manner, the milk should be set in the pure atmosphere of the sweet, well-kept milk house or cellar. For deep setting, the temperature should be kept at forty-five degrees, and at sixty or sixty-two for the shallow pan method. After about twenty-four hours, the cream should be removed from the deep pails, while the shallow pans should be allowed to stand about twelve hours longer. The cream thus obtained has become only slightly sour. Whenever you add fresh cream to the jar, the whole should be stirred, in order that it may ripen evenly. It is also well to state here, that every utensil used should be kept bright and clean by constant scrubbing and scalding.

| BEST DAIRY PAIL | The most approved milking bucket is made of double plate tin, with a heavy galvanized ring around the bottom. The

top of the pail should be with a rounded half cover to

MILKING BUCKET.

keep the dust out, and be finished with a strainer lip holding very fine wire gauze.

| DAIRY PAN | The dairy pans in former use were with a seam around the bottom, which gave opportunity for the sour milk to collect, and unless removed with great care, injured the flavor of the butter. This is now entirely gotten rid of by the newer pressed seamless pan, which is easily cleaned and keep sweet.

| PAIL RACK PAN DRYER | Among minor dairy appointments, is the simple and useful pail rack for sunning and drying the pails used in milking. Nothing sweetens utensils like this open-air process, for

which our great-grandmothers availed themselves of the pickets of the garden fence. For shallow pans, is presented a pan dryer, which is much the same thing as the rack for pails, allowing them to stand on the side, exposing both inner and outer surfaces to light and air.

| ROTATING SHELVES | A very convenient arrangement for the shallow pan system, is a set of revolving shelves, circular in shape, and turning on pivots fastened in the floor, and again in the ceiling. These save many steps in putting in the filled pans, and

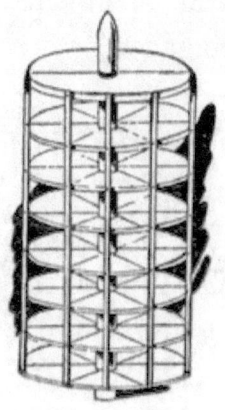

REVOLVING SHELVES.

also in skimming the cream from them, as the person can stand in one place, and accomplish either by simply turning the shelves.

THE PATENT CLOSET — This is another patent accepted by dairymen as especially adapted to the deep pail setting in a limited way. It has an ice chamber and drain, and is lined with zinc throughout.

PATENT CLOSET.

CHURNING — Churning is simply mechanical, and the way of turning cream into butter in the churn is too well understood by the practical dairyman to make it necessary to give it here in detail. It is more important to review the simple rules we have touched upon in the first part of this chapter, than to unnecessarily say very much on this subject.

44 PRATTS POINTERS ON COWS, SHEEP AND HOGS

CHURNS | A word on this subject might be of value to the beginner, who has much to learn from the experience of others. Fortunately, the tedious up-and-down dasher churn is a thing of the past and no longer used by the progressive dairyman. Many valuable patent churns are now presented,

MOTION OF CHURNS.

and all cover about the same ground in their motion and effect upon the cream. To more fully illustrate the motion of particular churns, see cut above, and it may be well to add that the bottoms of all improved churns are rounded, instead of square, making them much easier to clean.

CHAPTER VII.

BUTTER, ICE SUPPLY, ETC.

AN IDEAL DAIRY
A famous butter-maker once said, that the secret by which she obtained the superior flavor of her butter, was neatness and plenty of fresh air—opportunities free to everyone. A very pretty picture is made by a perfectly appointed dairy; for instance, a dairy surrounded by sweet green clover, and so clean, that a lady could go about it in a silk gown and lace cuffs. The milk house of stone, a clear spring bubbling close by the door, and sure to be cold on the hottest day. The pool inside, to hold on its stone slabs, earthen crocks covered with golden cream. A great bowl on the stone table holding the newly churned butter to be worked over in the early morning. Ivy and roses around the barred windows, through which creeps the cool air from clover-scented fields. In England the dairy business is often conducted by women, and yields generous returns for their industry and the money invested.

MAKING READY FOR THE MARKET
It has been already shown that proper feeding and care of the cow, management of the milk, correct temperature in raising the cream, etc., are essential points to insure good

butter. These influence its quality, texture, color and flavor, and not one of them can be disregarded, if a choice product is desired. When the "butter comes," a dairy term used to express its granulated state in the churn, it must go through several processes to make it fit for the market. The first and most important is to draw off the buttermilk, and pour cold water in the churn. By a few moves of the dasher, the butter can be washed free from every particle of buttermilk, which, if left, will be injurious to its flavor and prevent its keeping well.

SALTING AND PACKING — Butter, to keep sweet for months, must be properly salted, and this is a very particular duty of the dairy, and to be done with skill and care. The salt must be pure, very fine, and used one ounce to the pound. This is worked in and left twenty-four hours, when the butter is drained from all surplus water and worked over again for packing. After the butter has been finally worked, it should be packed at once, as exposure to the air will injure its quality. If sent to market in fancy prints, it is best to wrap each one separately in paraffine paper and pack them in a tight box, to be shipped without delay. For family use, the five-pound pail of spruce or maple veneer is a favorite method with purchasers. It should have a cover and handle. The inside is coated with paraffine, making it air-tight, and when packed, a sheet of paraffine paper covers the top before the wood cover goes on.

Butter pails and boxes should never be used for packing a second time, as they invariably give an unpleasant flavor to the best product, and may, therefore, be given to the buyer, out and out. The farmer who wishes to secure fancy prices and establish a reputation for superior gilt-edged butter, will wisely avail himself

PACKING BUCKET.

of tasteful styles in putting it on the market. The neat, attractive package, containing a week's supply, often commands a dollar a pound, while in reality the quality may be no better than that sold at one-half the price. With some families, dainty appearance and the guarantee of a certain name, goes a long way, and the dairyman is fortunate who can gain and cater to this class of trade. June butter is better adapted to keep a longer time, than that made at any other season of the year. It should be well packed in air-tight firkins, tubs or pails and kept in the ordinary temperature of a good cool cellar or milk house. Cold storage is most effective, but to prove successful must be conducted by a person who understands the business. By use of ice, the temperature varies, and if it falls too low, and is raised to a higher degree, decomposition takes place in the butter, which cannot be restored to its former condition, and is very difficult to stop. Therefore, a low, even, natural temperature of a cool cellar or spring house, is much better and safer for purposes of the private dairy.

| SUPPLY OF ICE | The dairy business requires a supply of ice in summer, and the farmer will find an ice house an economy, and a necessary convenience, and not a difficult matter to build and fill. |

FAMILY DAIRY ICE HOUSE.

A pond of clean, pure water, from which to cut ice in winter, a well-built house to store it, and dry, clean sawdust to pack it in, are the only requirements for success. The house should be constructed with non-conducting walls, a dry foundation and plenty of ventilation in the roof. To describe the method of building in detail, is unnecessary, as it is already well known. The ice house for the family can be erected at greater or less expense. We submit an ice house which is inexpensive, but very pretty.

CHAPTER VIII.

CREAMERY—MILK DAIRY.

PRIVATE OR STOCK CREAMERIES
There are two sorts of creameries, and either one of them is an advantage to a community where many cows are kept. The private creamery is the business of one man, who

MODERN CREAMERY.

purchases the cream of his neighbors at a stated price, taking his own risk as to labor and profit; the other is a joint-stock concern, the capital furnished by sale of shares. The stockholders govern the business, but employ persons competent to run it. The cream is bought from the farmers, who are glad to be relieved of the labor and care of butter-making. The butter product of a general creamery is usually superior in quality, as it is to the interest of the company to employ only experts in its manufacture. The illustration herewith shows a modern creamery. The creamery system is available

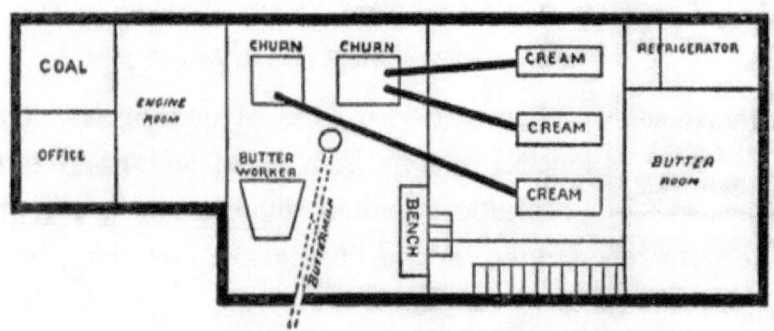

FIRST FLOOR OF CREAMERY.

for the large, private dairy, but its greatest development is reached by a stock company. In this way the product of several hundred cows can be worked up, and fifty or more farmers become regular patrons. Deep setting requires least space, and is, therefore, the system generally selected for the creamery. That co-operation is economy, finds proof in the cost of a six hundred cow creamery, here given from actual estimate. The necessary apparatus, including complete appointments for the making of butter and cheese, together with an eight horse-power boiler, can be erected from about $400 to $1,600. This affords capacity sufficient to make from eight to twelve hundred pounds of butter a day.

THE MILK DAIRY.

BEST COWS FOR THE MILK DAIRY The cows most desirable for the milk dairy are the half-bred Short-horns, grade Holstein, or Ayrshires. The Short-horns fatten easily when they are no longer profitable in their yield of milk. The Holstein and the Ayrshires are

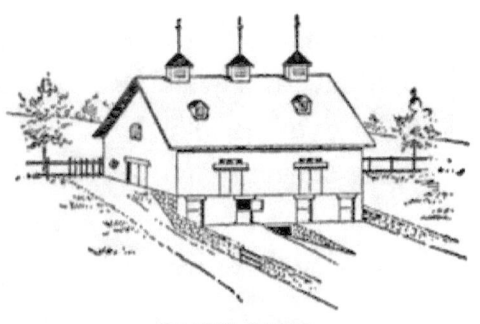

DAIRY BARN.

good beef cattle. All three are excellent milkers, both in quality and quantity. A dairy barn, holding about two hundred cows is here presented. The daily rations to give to this number of cows are a half-bushel of fresh brewers' grains mixed with a portion of corn-meal, and in addition to this, six quarts of dry yellow corn-meal, with the usual quantity of Pratts Food, and as much hay as they wish to eat. When brewers' grains are not fed, the ration of corn-meal is increased to twelve quarts daily, with hay. Adjoining the stable, which is kept scrupulously clean, is a spring house, in which the milk is rapidly cooled and kept until time to ship it. In summer the cows are pastured, but notwithstanding this, get their usual portion of corn-meal and Pratts Food. The principal crop fed is corn fodder, which is grown in long drills and carefully cultivated.

WHAT THE MILK DAIRYMAN MUST KNOW This business is disposing of the milk product to consumers, without further labor or expense in manufacture of butter and cheese. It is estimated that every family of five persons use at least one quart of milk a day, and at this rate more than a million cows would be required. Persons must fully understand the business of transporting and distributing milk to give it to customers in good condition. Three very important points are to be considered: first, to produce an excellent quality of milk;

second, to practice the best methods of caring for it, and third, how to dispose of it at the largest profit, and also how to give satisfaction in its delivery to buyers. These are absolutely necessary for success in the business.

COOLING THE MILK Cooling the milk properly, is of the utmost importance, and is more successfully done by putting it at once in the cans and submerging them in a tank of cool water. Fifty degrees is about the right temperature, and, as with the butter dairy, neatness is absolutely essential in the care of milk for market. The morning milk is shipped at evening for early delivery next day, and the evening's milk is shipped at the same time, but not mixed in the cans.

MILK ROUTE AND TRANSPORTATION The cows are milked at five o'clock in the morning, and the milk is at once strained into twenty-quart cans and kept in a cool place until shipped. If sent in bulk, these cans are sent in a milk can box, which can be padded in winter to prevent freezing, and in summer a centre can of pounded ice put in with the milk. Bottling milk, is a neat and convenient way of serving it, and is very generally used on the best milk routes. The milk is strained, cooled and sealed tightly in glass cans, by means of rubber

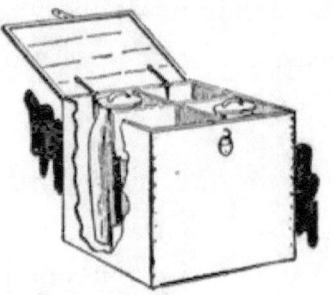

FOR SHIPPING MILK.

rings under the glass covers. Two excellent cans of this sort are here shown. Every milkman should have cards

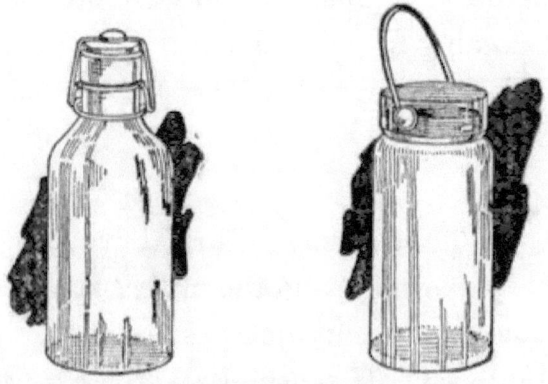

GLASS CANS.

of direction printed, and supply them to each customer, and in this manner insure proper care of his product after it leaves his hands. The card generally reads as follows: "Keep this bottle in a cool place. When empty rinse in cold water, fill again with cold water and let stand until called for." This precaution protects the reputation of the milk, and doubly pays for the trouble and expense of the cards to the dairyman. This bottling system saves the milkman the trouble of measuring, as every can holds either a pint or quart exactly. It is a convenience to the customer, as the milk can be received without taking pitcher or pail when the milkman rings, and is temporarily safe from dust or disturbance if left before the household is yet stirring in the early morning.

CHAPTER IX.

DISEASED MILK.

Milk is quickly affected by various diseases of the udder, and also by constitutional disturbances. These changes in milk are significant and not to be disregarded by the dairyman, who should at once inform himself of the cause, and how best to correct it.

BLUE AND WATERY MILK Excellent milk often has a bluish tint, but is a very different fluid from that watery, blue milk, which is regarded as a sure and distinctive symptom of the fatal disease called tuberculosis. It is infectious, and in every instance renders the milk unfit for food. The worst effects are produced upon persons using it, and to infants it proves a sure poison. The opinion of a skilled veterinarian should decide upon the condition of the milk and its probable cause, and if tuberculosis, the cow should be killed at once, and buried deep to avoid all danger in the future.

MILK SICKNESS This is a disease that is very peculiar, inasmuch as the infected cow does not suffer from it. Calves and persons using the milk, sicken and often die from slow poison in consequence. Male cattle will contract the sickness and die from it, while cows seem to escape all evil effects, the poison passing off in the milk. Many different theories are advanced as to the cause of milk sickness in certain localities, none of them accepted as thoroughly reliable. To avoid using milk, butter, cheese and meat from places where the disease is known to exist, seems the only sure protection. Bacteria, now charged with almost every evil, is credited with this also by eminent scientists. The treatment consists of stimulants and correctives wisely administered. Pratts Food is a mild stimulant, and is found in such cases to be most valuable.

VICES OF COWS A cow properly treated from the first is always gentle and without troublesome habits. The dairyman who breeds his herd can control this, as no truer proverb exists than that many owners spoil the cow. The chief faults of the dairy cow are kicking, holding up her milk and self-sucking, all of them very provoking. Patience, kindness and a gentle but firm rule, is about the most effective treatment by which these habits can be corrected.

Kicking is probably the worst, because the most wasteful fault of the cow, and can most always be entirely cured by kind words and a little petting. If this does not answer, the milker must not lose patience, but try a sharp cut or two with a rawhide, which will teach a lasting lesson. In case it does not stop the habit, tie a rope in a slanting position all way around the body just in front of the udder and just in front of the tail. A cow tied this way will not kick. Holding up the milk seldom occurs with cows whose calves are removed at birth and brought up by hand, as is now the generally approved method in the best dairies. Many ways to overcome this habit have been tried, but none better than soothing words, petting and perseverance. If the case continues obstinate, refuge is found in the silver milking tube.

The self-sucking cow is enough to try the temper of anyone. It is a habit contracted at any age, old or young, and if not broken entirely, destroys the animal's usefulness as a dairy cow, and renders her an expense instead of a profit to her owner. When everything else fails, slitting the tongue at the end for about two inches makes the action of suction impossible. Cruel as this way seems, it proves about the only remedy after the habit is once firmly established.

CHAPTER X.

READ THIS CAREFULLY.

NOTE In treating on diseases, we have endeavored in all cases to give in our judgment, the very best remedies, and where Pratts Food is named we consider it the *best for the case*, and in our actual practice we should use it and no other.

At the same time, as this book is intended to be a standard work of general information upon cows, sheep and hogs, we specify other remedies in addition to Pratts Food, preferring to give other information in our possession, thereby allowing the reader the choice of remedies.

We feel it advisable to specially call attention that

Pratts Food is known as the greatest *Animal Regulator* of the present day. It is a strictly up-to-date article, and is used and endorsed by many thousands throughout the United States, Europe and other foreign countries.

Every package is sold under our affidavit, guaranteeing its freeness from poisons or other injurious ingredients. It is pure and wholesome, and can be used without the least fear of bad results that often follow many condition powders and unreliable Foods.

It controls and regulates the blood, bowels and digestive organs; acts as a mild tonic and stimulant, and thereby cures and prevents the many diseases arising from these causes, and is used with greater success than any known preparation.

Its composition is of roots, herbs and barks of the best quality only. It is manufactured with the greatest care and exactness; the utmost cleanliness is observed.

It is quick in action, safe to use and a high-grade preparation in every particular.

In mixing Pratts Food with the feed, at first it may be well to dampen it. When fed dry, however, be careful to see it does not sift through the feed and lie uneaten at the bottom of the trough. After the animals become acquainted with the flavor, they are quite fond of it and eat it with a relish.

In all cases where the animal is too sick to eat, make a gruel of Pratts Food, by mixing with warm water, and pour down the throat; where quick movement of the bowels is necessary, it can be given in large doses at first, then gradually reduce size and lengthen time between the doses, and as the animal recovers mix the Pratts Food with the regular feed and discontinue the gruel. After the necessary movement of the bowels, (in cases of sick animals,) the quantity of Pratts Food should be reduced to the amount necessary to keep the bowels natural and regular. The gruel form of feeding Pratts Food is only required: first, when the animal needs prompt action of the bowels; second, when the animal is too sick to eat; or third, when the condition of the animal requires prompt or more than ordinary treatment. In all other cases, Pratts Food should be fed by mixing it with the regular feed.

The constant feeding of Pratts Food keeps live stock in such excellent condition that they are not liable to disease. Many dairies are kept entirely free from all sickness by its constant use as a dairy food. Its equal is unknown for standing bulls and stallions. It more than pays for itself many times over. Oxen are healthy and grow larger where it is fed; their meat is finer flavored. Calves grow quickly, robust and healthy. It frees swine from all diseases and makes the raising of them profitable. Prevents and positively cures hog cholera, except in its last stages. Sheep fed on Pratts Food pay largely. Lambs are strong and free from disease. As a horse regulator it is endorsed by all. Full directions for feeding Pratts Food are found in every package.

Pratts Food for Horses and Cattle, Sheep and Hogs is endorsed as the greatest *Animal Regulator* known in the world. And is the only Animal Regulator used and sold throughout the world.

CATTLE DISEASES.

THE DAIRY COW

The cow is a hardy, healthy animal, and if properly fed and cared for, is subject to very little sickness. The dairy cow, when fed judiciously, will frequently last twenty years, but this cannot be expected if she suffers from neglect, carelessness or cruelty. The Jersey cow, while high-bred and valuable for her remarkable products of milk and butter, is not as robust, but far more delicate than the ordinary dairy cow. Notwithstanding this, she is a favorite with the dairyman, and often purchased as the family cow. "Prevention is better than cure," and, therefore, the farmer should take the greatest care to avoid all existing or exciting causes of illness, and be quick to detect and prompt to remedy approaching trouble. A healthy animal shows unmistakable signs of its condition—the eyes are bright, coat smooth, appetite good, breathing regular and milk given in full measure. The sick cow has more or less fever, failing appetite, hot muzzle and rapid breathing. The soft eyes become dull, the hair rough, and all these symptoms rapidly increase, becoming more marked, unless the cause is determined and relief obtained. Illness usually arises from overfeeding, exposure and sudden cold, in which immediate action must be taken. Animals are patient and without complaint until sickness is firmly fixed upon them. Only constant vigilance of the farmer can keep the dairy herd in good condition. To do this is to his interest and profit.

INFLAMMATION OF THE LUNGS

Is caused by over-exertion or exposure, and is noticeable by a shivering, droopy appearance, loss of appetite and feverishness. The action of the lungs is quite rapid, and the breathing short, of a panting character. The cow generally goes dry after being attacked, and in very bad cases, the animal stands with legs wide apart, and with the nose pointed toward the window or door, as if trying to get fresh air. It generally gets hide-bound, the muzzle is hot and the nostrils scarlet. Blankets wrung out in hot water should be continually applied to the chest and sides, and a blister of turpentine and mustard may also be applied. The treatment must be quick. If it is necessary to move the bowels, large doses of Pratts Food should be given in gruel form. After the bowels move freely, reduce the size of dose and lengthen the time between doses. When the animal commences to eat, mix the regular quantity of Pratts Food in each feed. In referring to note on page 58, you will find we mention our intention to give other remedies as well as Pratts Food, so we name the following remedy to be given every three hours, first, however, giving one quart of castor oil to move the bowels: Twenty drops Tincture of Aconite; four drachms Carbonate of Ammonia ; two drachms of Belladonna. Mix thoroughly in one pint of water.

PLEURISY.

This is produced by the same causes that produce inflammation of the lungs. It will be noted especially by the character of the breathing. There will be extreme tenderness of the muscles of the chest, also a jerky movement by the abdominal muscles. There is also a marked tenderness between the ribs, which can be noted by pressing the animal there. Sometimes the water has to be drawn from the chest, which, however, requires the services of a veterinarian, and should not be done by one not knowing how to go about it. Pleurisy yields very quickly to prompt administration of Pratts Food, which should be fed in gruel form if the animal is too sick to eat. The same blister applications, etc., as mentioned for inflammation of the lungs should also be used. Our note on page 58, explains that we will give other treatments as well as Pratts Food, so we mention the following recipe: Twenty drops Tincture of Aconite; three fluid ounces Acetate of Ammonia. Mixed in one pint of water.

BRONCHITIS.

This disease is an inflammation of the larger tubes of the lungs. It is always accompanied by a cough. There is a dullness and drooping of the spirits, loss of appetite, mouth hot and dry, nostrils scarlet or reddish brown. The cough is at first harsh, and then followed by a whitish discharge from the nose, and then becomes more soft and rattling. You will notice the discharge from the nose about the third or fourth day. The animal generally lies down. It should be kept in a warm stable and fed soft food and have good care. Pratts Food in large doses in form of a gruel, sufficient to physic the animal, should be given and then the quantity reduced to the regular amount. Sometimes warm water injected into the bowels helps recovery. The front of the throat or chest may be blistered, or hot water cloths applied and then covered with blankets. The nose bag, recommended for horses, is a mighty fine thing, and often effects a rapid recovery, along with the constant use of Pratts Food. Note on page 58 says that we would in all cases mention other recipes, so we mention the following: Three fluid ounces Acetate of Ammonia; one-half fluid drachm Tincture of Squills. Mixed with one pint of water.

COLDS.

They are generally noticed by a heated forehead and sneezing of the animal. Very frequently there is a cough, sometimes diarrhœa, much fever and loss of appetite. At other times, the animal is constipated and deficient in urine. In cases of severe illness, liberal quantities of Pratts Food in gruel form are all that is necessary, gradually reducing as the animal recovers. Many persons have home remedies which they apply according to their judgment. The animal should be kept warm and legs bandaged. Other local outward applications, as given for pleurisy and inflammation of the lungs, will also be found useful.

OVERLOADED PAUNCH.

Any kind of food will produce this trouble if taken too freely. It is slower to develop than bloat. The left side is distended and hangs downward. There is difficulty in breathing and stupor. It is caused by grain food. Diarrhœa sets in before death as a rule. Where Pratts Food is properly fed, this disease never occurs, and large doses of Pratts Food is a true remedy. If movement of the bowels is required very quickly, we mention: One pound Epsom Salts; one pound Glauber Salts; two fluid ounces Oil of Turpentine; one-half drachm Nux Vomica. Mixed thoroughly.

The above can be given along with the *usual* dose of Pratts Food, and is simply mentioned as a rapid purgative, but we would not recommend its use unless the animal is really suffering from severe costiveness and quick movement must be had, as Pratts Food, in gruel form, will move the bowels, but takes a little longer time than the above.

MAD STAGGERS.

This is caused by a feverish condition of the system, also by eating dry grain husks or bleached hay, which collects in hard lumps and which can be felt by pressing the right side with the closed fist. The dung is scanty and hard, yet maybe at first, the animal will have diarrhoea. The animal lies on the left side, with head turned to right flank. Paralysis, stupor or convulsions may follow, or mad delirium so bad that the animal may dash straight ahead, regardless of any obstacles, sometimes breaking its horns. Give a purgative immediately. A quart of castor oil will do, and at once commence with double quantity of Pratts Food. Repeat the castor oil in eight hours if the first dose does not move the bowels. An injection of warm water into the bowels will help to move them quickly if the disease is so far gone that you cannot wait for the castor oil to act. The food should be gruel and soft foods. However, as per our note on page 58, we give this additional recipe: Four drachms of Carbonate Ammonia every three hours.

INFLAMMATION OF THE BOWELS.

This is caused by irritating food, also a change in the water. You will find at times that dung may be passed in small balls streaked with blood; the animal will suffer much pain and rush recklessly about. Sometimes it is caused by eating poisonous plants, the urine in this case will be high-colored and often bloody. Mucus may be found in the dung instead of blood. There will be belching of gas and bad breath. Diarrhoea may start, which will either cure the animal or cause it to die quickly. In case of extreme pain, two ounces of laudanum may be given by injection or in the mouth to ease the pain. In very bad cases, blankets wrung out in hot water may be applied to the abdomen. Pratts Food, mixed with a warm gruel every two hours, is the best feed to give first, and after that soft feed mixed with Pratts Food should be given for some weeks. Our plan of giving another remedy, as per note on page 58, leads us to mention the following: Carbonate of Ammonia, four drachms; Extract of Belladonna, two drachms. Give in warm gruel every two hours.

DIARRHOEA—SCOURS.

Large doses of Pratts Food in necessary quantities to physic the animal is all that is needed. If the animal is too sick to eat, make a gruel of Pratts Food mixed with warm water and pour down the throat. After which, continue with the Pratts Food together with starchy foods, gruels and mashed roots. In chronic diarrhoea, Pratts Food is invaluable. In case it continues too long, the animal should be killed, and buried deep, and should not be eaten under any circumstances nor fed to the hogs. As per our plan to furnish another recipe (see note on page 58), we give the following: Two fluid drachms of Tincture of Kino. Three times daily.

DYSENTERY.

In its first stages, the dung is semi-fluid and of bad odor ; later contains blood and mucus and is very offensive. Discharges are very painful and straining. The appetite is lost, hair staring and thirst is great. There is much fever. Pratts Food in large doses (in gruel form if the animal cannot eat), sufficient to physic, is all that is necessary. Afterwards continue usual size doses. However, as we have frequently mentioned, we purpose giving in all cases another recipe, as per note on page 58, and therefore mention : Two ounces pulverized inner bark White Oak ; two fluid ounces Oil of Turpentine. Mixed with one quart of water or gruel. This should be given twice daily.

SCOURS IN CALVES.

This is simply indigestion. It is noted by poor appetite, or a very ravenous appetite, a bloated pot belly, staring hair, bad breath and watery diarrhoea. The calf soon becomes emaciated and dies. A good thing to do, is to give two fluid ounces of castor oil with a teaspoonful of laudanum, and then feed Pratts Food in gruel form regularly. We advise castor oil only when a quick physic is required; if the case is not an extreme one, we would not advise giving it. If it is a sucking calf, be sure and feed the cow Pratts Food, as it is always well to treat the cow same as the calf during the time of sucking.

COLIC.

One pint of Glauber salts dissolved in pint of warm water should be first given, and afterward inject a quart of warm water in the bowels, with two fluid ounces of laudanum added to it. Then feed regularly Pratts Food, mixed with warm water as a gruel, if the animal is too sick to eat. Colic does not occur when Pratts Food is fed regularly. We would advise blankets wrung out in hot water to relieve the pain. In extreme cases, especially if there is nervous excitement, give, next in value to Pratts Food as a remedy (see page 58), the following: Four drachms of Carbonate of Ammonia; two drachms of Belladonna. Mixed with one pint of water.

WORMS.

We can simply say nothing different from Pratts Food for these troublesome pests, which will surely and quickly rid the animal of same. Some feed tobacco, which is very good in its way. See note page 58.

CHOKING.

When the animal gets an object in its throat which it cannot pass, it will be noticed by staring eyes, great distress and rapid swelling of the stomach. Such obstructions can most generally be removed by pushing them down with the hand, of course, at the same time, properly securing the jaws so they are kept wide apart.

INFLAMMATION OF THE KIDNEYS.

This often occurs from eating poisonous plants or decayed food. It sometimes occurs right after calving. It will be noted by slight shivering, increased heat, the animal attempts to urinate frequently and passes but little, which is high-colored flecked with blood. By pressing on the loins, it will cause the animal to shrink on account of those parts being so tender. There is stiffness in the hind legs and a straddling gait. In extreme cases it may be well to cause quick action of the bowels by administering one and one-half pints castor oil mixed with two fluid ounces of laudanum. Follow this by free use of Pratts Food. In ordinary cases simply use at first large doses of Pratts Food, then reduce to regular quantity without the castor oil. Blankets wrung out in hot water may be applied to the loins for several hours, followed by a blister. Fluid food should be given until the danger is passed.

INFLAMMATION OF THE BLADDER.

This is noted by frequent passage of urine; there will be a twisting of the tail, uneasiness of the hind parts, straddling gait and slight fever. Pratts Food in large doses can be given so as to move the bowels, which is all that is necessary in these cases. This should be fed in gruel form if cow is too sick to eat; if not, mix with regular feed. Sometimes the disease is noticed in cows right after calving, and extreme costiveness of the bowels in such cases may be relieved quickly by a dose of castor oil. Inflammation of the bladder is cured and prevented by the use of Pratts Food, and calving is made freer and cleaner.

RED WATER

Is a constitutional ailment as a rule. Proper treatment is change of food, followed by same treatment as mentioned for inflammation of the kidneys. Feed on mashes until the animal gets better. Pratts Food prevents and cures red water, and is certain and quick.

ABORTION IN COWS

Is caused by either of the following: herding together of large numbers of cows, high feeding, crowded space, smutty corn and ergoty pastures or accidental injuries. Frequently when one cow aborts in a herd, others will follow from sympathy or infectious nature of the disease. The cow which has aborted should be immediately removed from the rest of the herd. When a case of this kind occurs, it is well to give all the animals in the herd Pratts Food. The sick animal should be fed on cooling food, such as soft mashes, etc. If there is any signs of weakness, Pratts Food (in gruel form where necessary, if animal is too sick to eat) will give the animal strength. If the case is very serious, to relieve the animal of pain only, a small dose of laudanum may be administered. In advanced stages, it may be necessary to remove the dead calf, for which a veterinarian should be called in. Where Pratts Food is fed constantly, it not only prevents the abortion in cows, but in all cases where instructions have been followed, it has stopped the abortion, and not only prevented the balance of the herd from aborting, but has built up the health of the affected cow. As per our note, page 58, we mention a recipe of one-half ounce of chlorate of potassa daily to be given to the well animals.

MILK FEVER.

This is generally caused by high fever before and after calving, running into rich pasture during hot weather; there is a feverish condition and inflammation of the brain; a complete stoppage of urine or dung. In the last stages, the cow goes into a state of stupor. Prevention is far better than cure in these cases, and proper care, and Pratts Food has invariably prevented anything like milk fever occurring. However, should this disease appear, for the benefit of those not feeding Pratts Food, we might mention that one pound of Epsom salts should be given to the cow so affected directly after calving, but to none others. Then feed Pratts Food and you will have satisfactory recovery of the animal in most all cases ; but another formula which we give for reasons stated in note on page 58, is as follows: Four drachms Carbonate of Ammonia; one scruple Nux Vomica. Mixed in one pint of water.

INFLAMMATION OF THE WOMB

Is generally caused by difficult calving or improper removal of the after-birth. It is noticed by shivering fits, colicky pains, uneasiness of the hind parts, twisting of the tail, looking toward the flank and frequent straining. The entrance to the vagina has a red inflamed appearance. If the hand is introduced, the womb will be found dilated with fluid which must be withdrawn by use of a small rubber tube, which should be followed by injections of warm water to clean the womb, and a teaspoonful of solution of carbolic acid, mixed with a pint of warm water, should also be injected. Sometimes a pound of sulphate of soda is good. However, a gruel of Pratts Food, should the animal be too sick to eat, is all that is necessary in cases of this kind, with proper care as mentioned above. After the animal has recovered, Pratts Food should be fed, mixed with its regular feed. The womb should be cleaned out every couple of days with the solution of carbolic acid and warm water, as mentioned above.

BLOODY MILK.

This is caused generally by injuries to the bag. Some cows show signs of it during heat. We would advise changing the regular food, feeding Pratts Food, and apply plenty of cold water to the bag, and be very careful in milking.

GARGET.

This occurs from too great a supply of milk-producing foods, or from local injuries. The bag may be hard and a lump felt in the centre. Cold water applications are a good thing, and Pratts Food (in gruel form where necessary) is all that is required. Active hand rubbing of the bag three or four times a day is good. Iodide of potassium in drachm doses is helpful. The milk must be drawn off frequently, and if painful, a milking tube must be used to allow it to run out.

TO PREVENT LEAKING OF MILK.

This may be prevented by taking white oak bark, put in water and boil down to a strong solution. After milking, soak ends of leaky teat in the solution for a few minutes.

PLEURO-PNEUMONIA.

This is generally noted in the sick animal by drooping head, arched neck, hollow flanks, dull-looking or staring coat and a general appearance of great dejection. The pulse is frequent, sometimes full, during the latter stages of the disease it is frequent. There is some little mucus at the nose and very high-colored urine, which is often retained for a long while until the bladder becomes very much distended. The cow stops giving milk in the early stages of the disease. There is costiveness and the breathing frequent, sometimes panting. The temperature of the body is from 107 to 109. There is a trembling and twitching of the muscles and unsteady gait. In advanced stages the animal lies down and has partial paralysis of the hind quarters, the hind limbs being drawn slightly under the belly and the fetlock joints bent as in other severe diseases. Sometimes the paralysis extends to the forelegs. We advise killing the animal at once. Pratts Food will, if fed in time, prevent this disease.

COW-POX OR VARIOLA.

This is a highly contagious, eruptive fever, communicated alike to mankind, horses and cows. Round inflamed spots appear upon the teats, (see illustration) and in three or four days fill with liquid, which afterward becomes thick yellow pus. This is the true vaccine-virus used by inoculation as an antidote for smallpox. The influence of cow-pox upon mankind is much the same as vaccination—a slight fever, swelling of the glands and headache. The disease spreads through an entire herd of dairy cows very rapidly, probably conveyed by the milkers, whose hands and clothing naturally become infected. This disease is not a dangerous one, neither is the treatment difficult,—the greatest care, however, must be taken not to break the pox, or they will make stubborn sores, troublesome to heal. To allay the constant irritation, soothing applications of cosmoline, vaseline or other coal-oil preparations may be used, together with Pratts Food, to regulate the general system. This should be given to all the cows and heifers not yet affected.

COW-POX.

APHTHA, SORES ON THE LIPS AND TONGUE.

This disease is confined to painful blisters, soon becoming sores on the lips and tongue, so that the cow cannot eat and grows weak, falling off in milk rapidly.

It yields readily to simple treatment. The mouth is washed twice a day with one ounce borax and one fluid ounce tincture of myrrh mixed in one quart of water. Pratts Food should be carefully fed to all the herd when aphtha first appears. If the mouth is too sore to permit the animal to eat freely, we would recommend a gruel of Pratts Food mixed with warm water, and then pour it down the throat and feed the animal on regular gruel feed.

OBSTRUCTED TEATS.

CAKED BAG TUBE.

Small tumors sometimes form and close the milk ducts, but in the same manner as a boil, they usually come to a head and break. At times, however, they make a permanent obstruction, which has to be removed with a probe, and the passage afterward kept open with a wooden plug until perfectly healed.

DEPRAVED APPETITE.

Cows will at times select rotten wood, old bones, rubbish, etc., as diet, which shows plainly that from irritation of the stomach, they are possessed of an unnatural appetite. Pregnancy, a diseased liver, tuberculosis, balls of hair and other foreign substances in the stomach will produce this condition, which should be treated as ordinary indigestion. Pratts Food is an excellent regulator of the appetite, and it should be fed in liberal doses to the sick animals.

PART II.

PRATTS POINTERS ON THE SHEEP.*

CHAPTER I.

GENERAL REMARKS ON SHEEP-RAISING.

ORIGIN OF SHEEP-RAISING
Sheep-raising is one of the oldest of man's industries. The herding of sheep dates back almost to the beginning of the world. In the early ages, the necessities for sustaining life were not so plentiful, so man turned quite naturally to the sheep for its wool to use in protecting his

---

*To obtain all the advantages of our remarks on the sheep, first read the note on page 58.

body, and the meat for his food. It does not cost much to keep sheep, when you think of the slight cost of the food and the great profit derived. They eat grass and cheap fodder, which is of little value unless used in this way, and return it threefold in their product of wool, mutton and manure. The sheep is not an animal adapted to endure hardship. Without proper food and shelter, the wool will lose its softness, the lambs born, prove weak and small, showing that to thrive, the sheep must be well cared for.

CHOOSING THE FARM The climate and the natural advantages which this country affords, to those who are thinking of raising sheep as a business, or on their farms, in connection with other work, is second to none. This occupation has been steadily on the increase of late years. Hilly farms are often a great source of labor for their owners from which they get little return, but when these same hills are turned into grazing land for the sheep, the profit is more than doubled. There is not so much need that the soil be rich, but the drainage is the all-important point. If the land is not drained naturally, artificial drainage has to be resorted to, and while this often costs a great deal, it will pay in the end. It is unwise to select pasture where pools of stagnant water exist, as animals drinking from them, become diseased in a very short time. A sandy or gravelly soil, uneven and hilly, with short grass generously mixed with clover, is particularly favorable to the sheep.

WATER SUPPLY

Sheep need fresh water, and in large quantities. A permanent spring or running stream is very convenient and economical, but a good well answers the purpose. Hard water is the best, that is, water that contains more or less lime and salt. These are good for the sheep's system.

GRASSES IN THIS COUNTRY

The farmer is very familiar with the more common grasses, such as Red Top, Kentucky Blue, Orchard Timothy, Oat-top and White Clover. These are the principal grasses in this country, and make excellent food for the sheep. The physical condition of an animal, whether good or bad, is shown by unmistakable signs which should not be disregarded by those responsible for its care. The wool of the well-fed and properly nourished sheep will be soft and very greasy, while that of the poorly fed animal will be dry and harsh to the touch. In the latter case, the diet should be changed and exposure to cold and bleak winds avoided. Peas, corn or oats cut and fed green, furnish excellent additional nourishment.

CARE OF THE SHEEP Years gone by, wolves and wild beasts were the worst enemies to sheep; at the present day dogs are their worst enemies, and the greatest possible care should be taken to protect

DOG GUARDS.

them from these creatures. This is easily accomplished by the use of "dog guards," a very simple contrivance

SHEEP SHED.

of wires easily attached and adjusted, which afford complete protection to the flock.

A well-built shed as shelter, should be provided for the flock even in summer. This is shown in a practical form in illustration here given. It does not cost much, and can be so located that each side will open into a separate pasture. Sheep enjoy roaming, and it is an acknowledged fact that they do not thrive as well, when kept in the same pasture on the same diet for any length of time. It is curious to note how sheep will select certain places in a pasture and crop them close, as if the herbage were sweeter and better there than elsewhere. In this way nature indicates the food they prefer and, as a rule, that which is best for them.

THE SICK SHEEP — When sick, an animal is guided by instinct to seek a remedy in the plant world. At such time it will eat, with eagerness and seeming relish, weeds and leaves with a very bitter and unpleasant taste. This fact convinced the shepherd of early times that he must depend upon wormwood and wild parsley as cures for all troubles of the sheep. The sheep-raiser of the present day finds in regular feedings of Pratts Food both prevention and cure, in a much more convenient and reliable form.

CHAPTER II.

CARE OF THE FLOCK IN WINTER.

NECESSARY BUILDINGS | The sheep must be comfortably sheltered in winter. A good barn or shed can be built for this purpose. It need not be an expensive structure, but should be placed on high, dry ground and have a tight roof and good floor.

SHEEP BARN.

The barn should have a loft for storing fodder, hay, etc., a ground floor with convenient feeding racks, and underneath a basement, containing a small cellar for

CHEAP SHEEP SHED.

keeping roots. Traps are so arranged in the loft that hay may be put in the racks from above. Sheep require a great amount of fresh air, therefore the barn is usually placed with its front to the south and without doors. Many farmers prefer a wide sliding door, however, which

HURDLE.

can be used in extreme weather to shut out the snow and wind. Below we give an illustration of an inexpensive sheep shed.

Many labor-saving inventions are now presented for use upon the sheep farm, among them the field hurdle,

SHEEP NETTING.

used to divide a pasture into strips, that it may be fed and fertilized evenly. A strong netting of hemp or cocoanut fibre is also furnished for the same purpose, and with shepherds in England, is considered more convenient than the wooden hurdles.

The portable hurdle, made from crossed sticks on a centre pole, can be lifted and moved at a moment's

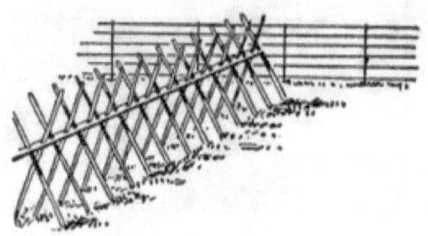

PORTABLE HURDLE.

notice, and is much used to shut in portions of the pasture for feeding, while those exhausted may be given opportunity to strengthen and grow again.

The practical farmer needs no description of the ordinary feed rack for sheep, but the new portable rack

PORTABLE FEEDING RACK.

deserves mention. It is long, narrow, and with two underneath wheels at each end, and handles in front. The top is covered with narrow strips of wood dividing it into feeding sections. It is moved with the same ease as a wheelbarrow, and intended to convey the cut roots to any part of the yard or pasture, and can also be used for hay or green fodder.

SHED FOR A FEW SHEEP | The farmer who keeps a small number of sheep, of course only needs a small shed. It can be built very cheaply, having a deep projecting roof and entirely open in front. The little yard that surrounds this shed should be enclosed by a fence. A pen is sometimes boarded up in one corner of the shed for the shelter of ewes with young lambs, who cannot endure the cold winds of early spring. Corn stalks, straw, forest leaves, sawdust, etc., make the best litter for the floor of the sheep barn or shed.

WINTER FOODS | Sheep, more than any other animals, enjoy a change of food and thrive better on it. The farmer has a great number of foods to select from when choosing food for the winter. He need only consider the market price of the food and the object of his sheep-raising. If rapid growth is desired, both in ewes and the lambs they produce, clover hay ranks first as a winter diet. Pea and oat straws also furnish nutritious food. Corn stalks form a better bedding than they do food. Sugar beet is undoubtedly the best feed for sheep and, when used in connection with dry fodder, furnishes almost a perfect diet; and turnips are also most nutritious.

To feed roots judiciously, the farmer must take into consideration the kind of sheep, their weight, etc. It is claimed as a safe rule that a bushel and a half of roots may be fed daily to fifteen sheep who weigh 150 lbs. each, and in connection with this may be given 1¼ lbs. of hay and ¾ lb. of bran to each animal. The sheep-raiser will gain the most available knowledge in reference to his flock by experience and constant watchfulness of cause and result. Grains are valuable as fattening food for sheep.

REGULARITY IN FEEDING

When sheep are taken from pasture in the fall and put upon a diet of dry fodder, great care must be taken that

ROOT CUTTER AND PULPER.

their health does not suffer from it. Machines for cutting up roots before feeding are now on the market.

When the roots are prepared in this manner, there is less danger of their choking. Better results will be given if the animals are fed regularly, and their appetites and digestion will be improved. Fresh water should always be kept where the sheep can get it when they want it. The sheep will thrive and grow faster when they are attended to properly.

CHAPTER III.

BREEDS OF SHEEP.

AMERICAN BREEDS The first sheep imported from England, were of a much better quality than the sheep which were imported from Spain. These were thin and the wool coarse. Some of this old stock though somewhat improved, can be found out on the plains of the West. The already greatly improved stock is being made better each year by the introduction of Leicester, Southdown and Cotswold blood.

CROSS-BRED SHEEP This is a breed of sheep in England and is explained thus: Certain breeds of sheep are noted for their fleece, and therefore, are kept especially as wool producers. These animals are of slow growth and mature late. Other breeds are distinguished by the choice quality and flavor of their meat, and are bred and raised for that product only. Mutton sheep, from feeding and fattening generation after generation, lose their strength of constitution, and after a time are not prolific. By crossing the wool-bearing and the mutton sheep, the cross breed is obtained, which possesses advantage over both. It unites quick growth and early maturity with a good quality of mutton and wool, is strong and hardy, and the lambs produced are thrifty and good size.

THE AMERICAN MERINO The American Merino ranks not only as the model sheep in this country, but in every other where its value has been tested. They are carefully bred. In the early part of this century, the consul in Lisbon purchased and sent to the United States several thousand sheep of the best pure breed in Spain. These were widely scattered all over the country and became the basis of many excellent herds. The wool is soft, oily and elastic to the touch, medium fine, and usually between two and three inches in length. (See illustration on back cover.) Some points in reference to wool are valuable to the sheep-raiser, among them, that the finest fleece is by no means the most profitable, as the present demand is for medium wool. It is claimed that the wool tester becomes so expert in his business that he can determine the relative quality and value of different fleeces when blindfolded.

THE SOUTH-DOWN | The many choice breeds of sheep in foreign countries cannot be described in the limit of this volume, but a few most used to improve the stock of this country will receive brief mention. The Southdown seems almost like a

SOUTHDOWN RAM.

native American stock. It thrives well in the ordinary farm, being strong and hardy. The finest early lambs are secured by crossing the Merino ewe with a pure-bred Southdown or Cotswold ram.

THE COTSWOLD — Like the Southdown, this breed seems like a native American. It suits itself very easily to the climate and also takes very kindly to the pasture.

COTSWOLD.

THE IMPROVED KENTUCKY
About fifty years ago, a Kentucky breeder, being desirous of improving his stock, carefully selected a number of the best ewes, and bred them with a Merino ram. The ewes from this cross were bred with an imported pure-bred Leicester, and their lambs in turn with the finest Cotswold. The Virginia sheep produce choice mutton, a long, fine fleece. The lambs are active, large and mature early, which are all points of the good sheep. This stock is now generally accepted, especially in the South and West, as excellent and reliable.

CHAPTER IV.

BREEDING.

THE RAM
Sheep-raisers, in choosing a ram, take into consideration its shape and the quality of its fleece. The model sire has a round body, short legs, broad loin, small head and close wool.

CARE OF THE EWE
The sheep carries her young five months, and should be bred so that the lambs will come in mild weather. During this time the ewe must be well fed and may be given small quantities of bran, oats or crushed corn. Pratts Food should

be fed in regular rations each day, in order to keep the sheep in good condition and to make the lambs strong and healthy. If this system of management is steadily observed, **the lamb will be dropped without trouble, the ewe will give an abundant supply of milk to nourish it and both will thrive astonishingly.** A sheep is not al-

HURDLE FOR EWES.

ways willing to nurse her offspring, but can be compelled to do so by a very simple arrangement, known to the sheep-raiser as a hurdle. It is simply a pair of bars between which the sheep is fastened in such a manner that the lamb can nurse, and she is unable to prevent it. In a few hours she will **become accustomed to her new duties** and offer no further resistance.

OBJECT IN KEEPING SHEEP The sheep-raising farmer must decide from locality and circumstance which product will yield the best profit. If he looks to the fleece as a return for his outlay and labor, he should choose a wool-bearing breed. Should the convenience of a neighboring market afford opportunity for the sale of mutton and early lambs, he must select animals with quality of large size, early maturity and easy fattening. In crossing, all these points should be carefully considered. The ewes selected from the very best in the flock, and the ram, of whatever breed, the finest pure bred. Probably one of the best mothers is found in an improved native ewe with a generous share of Merino or Southdown blood in her veins. The ram may be pure-bred Cotswold, Southdown or Shropshire, as is most convenient.

CLEANLINESS AND COMFORT NECESSARY — Sheep will not thrive unless properly protected from cold and damp. They must be kept in clean pens and provided with plenty of clean, dry straw for bedding, or disease will appear in the flock. Precaution is better than a cure, applies particularly to sheep, who when given the right sort of care are seldom sick, but if neglected are subject to numberless diseases difficult to cure. Lambs are hardy, active little creatures when properly managed, and will grow and fatten very quickly under favorable surroundings. Animals sick and weakly from birth do not pay for the expense and trouble in raising, and should never be used to breed from; the stock will retrograde rather than improve. It costs no more to feed a good flock than a poor one, and there is a wide difference in the financial result.

FEEDING LITTLE LAMBS — In instances where the mother dies and the lamb is too young to drink milk from a basin, it can be readily taught to nurse from a sponge placed in the spout of the ordinary tin teapot. The milk of the ewe is very rich, and the best

FEEDING LAMBS.

substitute for it is found in slightly sweetened cow's milk warmed to the temperature when first drawn from the udder.

CARE OF THE LAMBS — A lamb is so innocent and confiding in its nature, that it suffers little neglect, but on the contrary is treated with great kindness by its care-takers. With all animals one fact is the same : whatever the kind or breed, if it proves profitable and successful, it must be well fed and properly cared for. If the lamb is to grow and mature early it should be given plenty of good food, and even while unweaned, additional nourishment may be added with benefit. If the ewes are kept in an enclosure the English method of arranging a small yard adjoining with

LAMB CREEP.

several openings, through which the lambs can enter and eat from little food boxes prepared for them, is a great convenience. Rye, oats and bran ground very fine make suitable feed for growing lambs.

WEANING LAMBS | Before this is attempted, the lambs must be able to eat well, and if possible should be put in pasture that they may learn to nibble the fresh, tender grass. They should not be removed from their mothers at once, but taken away during the day and allowed to nurse at night, and in this way the supply of milk will lessen gradually so that the ewes will not suffer any discomfort. The lambs eating for themselves will soon forget their mothers. At this time, it is very important that the ewes receive the best care and to dry the milk without trouble or fever.

CHAPTER V.

DISEASES COMMON TO SHEEP.

CAUSES, SYMPTOMS, PREVENTION AND CURE.

Before treating on the above, however, we refer you to the note on page 58, which it would be well to look over carefully before reading our remarks in reference to diseases of sheep.

Sheep are generally healthy animals, and few cases of sickness occur when they are properly taken care of. When neglected or improperly fed, however, like all other animals, they develop many ailments which frequently prove fatal unless promptly attended to. The symptoms of disease can be seen far enough in advance by careful watching, so that very few cases need prove fatal if the proper remedies are applied at the right time.

BRONCHITIS.

In this disease there is an inflammation of the air passages, and if not promptly checked, inflammation of the lungs will follow. The symptoms are very much like catarrh, only the cough is more severe and there is some fever and loss of appetite. The treatment in this case is Pratts Food, if very severe, in gruel form, and gradually reducing the dose and the length of time between doses, until the animal is in shape to eat, and then mix with the regular feed.

At the same time, as per our note so frequently referred to on page 58, we give the following: One drachm saltpetre, one drachm powdered gentian, and one ounce linseed oil, given for three or four days.

PLEURISY.

This is an inflammation of the membrane surrounding the lungs, and is very acute and painful. It is caused by exposure, low condition of the system and is not contagious; but many animals of the same flock often are taken sick because they are all likely to be subjected to the same lack of care or exposure which causes it. Prevention is much better than cure, and by proper care pleurisy should be prevented. We advise

Pratts Food; if the animal is very sick, in gruel form in large doses to move the bowels, and gradually decrease until the bowels are in good shape, when it can be mixed with the regular feed.

However, we give the following, as per note on page 58: One drachm nitrate of potash, one scruple of powdered digitalis and two drachms spirits of nitre. Give twice a day for four or five days, but first move the bowels freely with castor oil or some other purgative.

INFLAMMATION OF THE LUNGS.

This disease frequently occurs from herding too many sheep together; then again it is the result of exposure or insufficient ventilation in the stable. The latter is most frequently the cause. The common form will be known by the sheep panting, heaving of the flanks, discharge from the nose and a cough.

Pratts Food, fed in gruel form in frequent doses, is a valuable remedy. As the sheep recovers, the time between the doses should be lengthened, and as the sheep commences to eat, it can be mixed with the regular feed. In all cases where Pratts Food is used, after the bowels are once freely moved, the dose should be regulated so that the bowels will be natural and regular.

As mentioned in our note on page 58 to furnish

other recipes besides Pratts Food in curing ailments of sheep as well as other animals, we would mention the following: Ten drops of fluid extract of gelsemium dropped on the tongue twice a day. One ounce of chlorate of potash in half a pint of flaxseed tea, given daily until the animal shows improvement. Keep the animal apart from the others, so that it may have rest and quiet.

CATARRH.

Generally caused by exposure to rains and stormy weather. It is noted by a discharge from the nostrils and sneezing and sometimes coughing. The sheep should be placed in dry quarters and given Pratts Food, first in gruel form, later mixing with the regular feed.

In accordance with our note on page 58, we, however, give the following remedy: Two ounces of composition powder in a quart of boiling water; allow it to stand an hour, and after straining it, add three ounces of sugar of milk, and give about three tablespoonfuls several times a day.

CONSTIPATION.

Usually caused by a change in food. Frequently when sheep are changed from green pasture to dry fodder. Passages are hard and dry, and the animal moans with pain while the bowels are being moved. Costiveness is bad and should not be allowed to continue. Where Pratts Food is fed, constipation does not occur. In cases of severe costiveness it should be given in large doses and then decreased gradually. If it is a very severe case, an injection of warm water and soapsuds should be made, which will give relief.

As mentioned in our note on page 58, we give the following formula: One teaspoonful fluid extract of leptandra, two ounces Glauber salts in half pint of thin gruel, and drench the animal well.

TUBERCULOSIS.

This is a fatal disease, as is well known. The animal should be killed at once and buried deep. The meat should not be eaten by either people or animals. The disease is too well known to elaborate on and too fatal to suggest any remedy.

GARGET.

This is inflammation of the milk glands, and will not occur if the milk is drawn should the ewe lose her lamb. Drawing the milk, bathing the udder with warm water and feeding Pratts Food is all that is necessary.

DIARRHOEA.

This usually occurs from sudden changes of diet, or damp and foggy weather. Liberal doses of Pratts Food should be given in gruel form to thoroughly cleanse the bowels, and then gradually decrease to a sufficient quantity to keep the bowels in proper condition, at which time it can be mixed with the regular feed. It should be attended to promptly, however, as it often proves fatal. As mentioned in our note on page 58 that we will give other formulæ, we mention the following: One gill scalded milk, one drachm hyposulphite of soda, and one ounce pulverized animal charcoal. To a lamb give one-half this quantity, and repeat as often as seems necessary.

RHEUMATISM.

This is recognized as a blood disease and, of course, affects the whole system. It is almost always caused by exposure to cold and wet weather and poor diet. It is noticed by failing appetite, swollen and stiff joints and general restlessness.

The swelling changes from one place to another. When it becomes chronic, it hardens the joints until the animal becomes helpless and must be killed. Pratts Food is invaluable in this sickness, but the sheep must be well protected from the cold and damp, and have plenty dry straw for bedding. The other formula, which we speak of giving in our note on page 58, would be as follows: Two ounces of Epsom salts, two drachms of spirits of nitre, one-half drachm of fluid extract of ginger. Oat-meal gruel is very good along with the ordinary feed. Care must be taken of the flock, for if it once becomes chronic it is very hard to get rid of it. Sulphate of potash and sulphuric acid, given in two-drachm and twenty-drop quantity respectively in one-fourth pint of water, is very good.

INFLAMMATION OF THE BOWELS.

This does not often occur, but when it does, it is generally caused by impure water or bad food. Again, it may come from sudden cold. The symptoms are red, watery eyes, bowels are inactive, breathing short and difficult, followed by fever and loss of appetite and flesh. We would advise large and liberal doses of Pratts Food, to move the bowels freely, and then gradually decrease until the bowels become natural, and mix with the regular feed. We give the following, however, in accordance with note on page 58: A dose of linseed oil, castor oil or Epsom salts to move the bowels, and then give the animal proper care and nourishment.

PINING.

This is a blood disease caused by lack of nutrition. Sometimes it attacks very healthy flocks. It generally appears after long rains. The sheep become suddenly dull and lie down; eyes water and heads are lowered; the skin shrivels, the wool assumes a bluish color and death soon follows. This disease never appears in hilly pastures; consequently, a change of locality is the proper relief. High, dry fields with the pasturage short brings quick recovery. The feeding of Pratts Food, as a tonic to build up the animal, will produce surprising results.

FOOT ROT.

This is caused by exposure in low, wet pastures. There is generally weakness of the system; and it is contagious. The sheep limps usually at first in one of its fore-feet, and very soon all four become swollen until unable to walk. Blisters form and finally a deep sore, and unless cured the entire hoof drops off. The sick animal should be separated from the rest of the herd at once and all the sheep examined. All the diseased part of the hoof should be cut away and the foot washed with carbolic soap in warm water. After this they should be bound up—the bandage first dipped in a mixture of three ounces of pyroligenous acid to one and a half ounces water. Pratts Food should be fed to help improve the general health of the sheep.

APHTHA.

This is known by blisters in the mouth and on the feet of the sheep. It is painful and difficult to cure. In fact, it is better, where one or two animals only are affected, to kill them and bury them in protection to the other sheep. We, of course, feel that if anything will help them, Pratts Food will. A purgative may be used, such as Epsom salts, and the mouth washed with one ounce of powdered alum, and one ounce tincture of myrrh in a quart of water. The feet should be washed with warm soap-suds and bound up in carbolic ointment. This treatment may effect a cure, but it is a very serious disease.

INFLAMMATION OF THE BLADDER

Is very often due to the feeding of too much cornmeal. It is noted by the retention of the urine and fever. Pratts Food regulates the kidneys and bladder and suppresses all inflammation, and has proved successful in this disease. Feed per direction by mixing Pratts

Food with the regular feed of the animal. However, as per our note on page 58, to give different recipes, we mention the following treatment: Bleeding from the neck and linseed oil in two-ounce doses until the animal shows improvement.

SHEEP TICK.

This can be treated in the same manner as the scab mite.

SCAB MITE.

This is a very small insect and bores into the skin, causing burning sensations. The sheep become restless and scratch frequently and bite at their wool. The skin will be white and covered with a yellow liquid. The wool falls out. If a white cloth is thrown over the animal, they are apt to leave the sheep and crawl on the cloth. They increase very rapidly, and active measures should be taken at once to rid the animal of them.

The sheep should be dipped in a liquid of saturated tobacco stems or coarse tobacco leaves. It is good to add a little sulphur to this solution. Boiling water should be poured on it and the sheep dipped when it becomes cool and held in the solution for a few minutes. Repeat this about once each five or six days. If precaution is taken to dip sheep this way, say two or three times a year, it prevents them from being affected by the scab mite.

SHEEP LOUSE

Has a small, yellow body with dark-brown stripes and a red head. It attacks the neck and under the forelegs. The same dip as mentioned above for the scab mite is all that is necessary, although some advocate using coal oil.

When sheep are kept in a good, healthy condition, they are generally free from all ailments, and also with the proper care, pasturage, etc., are free from insects of all kinds, and therefore, if Pratts Food is fed constantly, and the liver, blood, bowels and kidneys kept in proper shape, you will experience a general, healthy condition of the whole flock.

POISON LAUREL.

Poisoning from laurel will be noticed by dullness, frothing at the mouth and blood-shot eyes. Action must be taken at once by injecting soap-suds in the bowels and giving a three-ounce dose of Epsom salts in warm water to each sheep. Then drench the animal well with warm water until it vomits. Injections of soap-suds should also be made. During recovery, to bring back strength to the animal, there is nothing as advantageous as Pratts Food.

WORMS

To which sheep are subject, can be readily and permanently cured, as well as positively prevented by the feeding of Pratts Food. There is generally a wasting away of the system, severe cough and rapid and difficult breathing from lung worms, and finally strangling of the animal. For this disease we would mention the free use of salt and fumes of turpentine.

Bladder worms are very troublesome, and sheep dying from this disease should be buried and not eaten by dogs or other animals. If not cured in its early stages, it is not likely to be. It is generally supposed to be caused by diseased dog's manure.

LAMBS.

Colic, diarrhoea, constipation, paralysis, water on the brain, and other ailments peculiar to lambs can be prevented, as well as cured, by the proper care of the ewe and the feeding of Pratts Food. The same treatment in all cases for the lambs, when large enough to eat, can be applied the same as for sheep, only in a modified form. Even paralysis is due to neglect in the care of the ewe and indigestion or depraved appetite caused by stomach troubles. Much might be said in reference to the different diseases of lambs, but intelligent reading of the diseases of sheep will enable the reader to comprehend the best method in handling any sheep disease that may occur in the flock.

PART III.

PRATTS POINTERS ON THE PIG.

CHAPTER I.

PROFITABLE PIG-RAISING

The man who raises pigs looks to their products as a return for the labor and money he expends; his whole object being to get, at the least cost, the greatest return of pork and lard from a certain quantity of food. In selecting the animals best suited to his purpose, he carefully considers the attention and food to be given them, as this is of the utmost importance in order to have the most successful results. Animals that grow quickly, mature early and fatten easily, are most desirable.

NATURE A GOOD TEACHER

A wise Providence bestows upon dumb animals a natural impulse which guides them, and serves in place of the sense to gain knowledge which man possesses. Cattle will eat and thrive on grass and hay, while the pig, when left to shift for itself, instinctively turns to acorns, roots, etc., proving that it requires a diet of less quantity and greater nourishment. This should be borne in mind when providing its food.

NECESSARY SURROUNDINGS

Comfort and warmth is a great influence upon the growth and health of animals. The pig will accommodate itself to circumstances more readily than any other domestic animal, but it is to the farmer's advantage to provide dry, warm pens and a liberal supply of food. If they are fed scantily and irregularly, they soon show the effect of neglect, and grow slowly, mature late and give poor return for whatever time and trouble has been given them.

ADVANTAGES

From every dwelling there is a daily amount of refuse, which, if not speedily disposed of, will accumulate and become burdensome, impregnating the atmosphere with foul and unhealthy odors, and would otherwise be thrown away. Hogs are great eaters and find excellent food in the scraps from the family table, parings of fruit, vegetables and the slops from the kitchen. They are of value to the dairyman ; and the farmer who feeds cattle with grains or oil cake, as he will be agreeably surprised to see how fat pigs will grow, when allowed to run in the barnyard and pick up the scattered leavings. This seems to decide that pigs are economical, useful and profitable on the farm if they are carefully selected and properly cared for.

RAPID GROWTH Self-preservation is the first law of nature, and this applies undoubtedly to animal life; therefore it is necessary to derive from daily food sufficient nourishment to sustain it, before flesh can be gained. If this is not done, life must depend upon matter already stored in the body. The pig, being better able to digest more food over and above the amount required to sustain life, gains more flesh in proportion to its size and amount of food eaten than any other stock. This affords a powerful argument in favor of liberal feeding, unless circumstances make it more convenient for the farmer to keep a large number of pigs, and let them mature slowly. For this purpose animals of slow growth should be selected for breeding, and the pigs fed on a moderate and limited allowance daily until they fully mature, and then they can be fattened quickly when desired for market.

PROPER CARE FOR EARLY MATURITY — It is to the interest and profit of the owner to see that his stock are provided with comfortable quarters. Hogs kept warm and sheltered will fatten on less food, than when exposed in open pens to storm and cold. It is wonderful to notice the improved appearance of pigs which have, for several generations, been kindly looked after and wisely managed. Each successive litter of pigs seems a better breed than the former ones,—the ears and snout more delicate, the legs shorter, the hair less coarse and the skin finer. It takes time to bring about this change, but the result is certain, when a steadfast system of liberal feeding and good care is maintained from year to year. Hogs, when neglected, will retrograde, becoming constantly less valuable, and transmitting to their young low habits and poor constitutions.

DEFINITION OF BREED — The word breed, as we use it, means "to nourish, to procreate, to originate." Certain characteristics develop in each litter of pigs, and if the breeder of pigs is careful to continue those conditions which influence them, they will become fully established and hereditary in each generation. The pig-raiser should be careful to choose a good stock to breed from, and then give them proper food and attention. Contrast the wild hog (which still exists in some parts of Europe) with the original old English pig, and you will surely be convinced that con-

OLD ENGLISH PIG.

ditions control breed. It must be admitted that while the latter is not a creature of beauty, as compared with the domesticated pig of to-day, yet it is a favorable change from the long tusks, rough hair, and strong snout of the wild hog. It required many generations of proper feeding and careful selection to change the black color, wicked disposition and many unfavorable traits of the wild creature, into the more quiet and domestic English pig. The best results were gained by crossing English sows with boars imported from China, and then selecting for breeding the young animals with the best points. All this required time and patience, but at last a profitable breed was fully established, and by crossing and re-crossing many times, other valuable breeds have been obtained.

THE MODEL PIG

It seems to be the aim of all the successful breeders to obtain a pig which is nearly of equal length, breadth and thickness, after having been properly fattened. To quote from

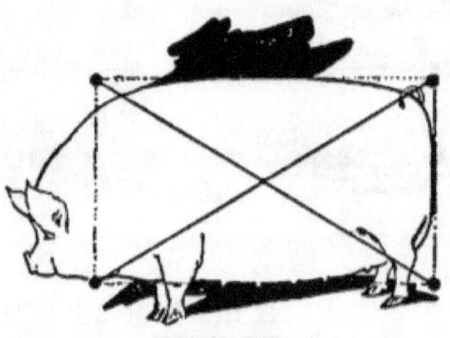

MODEL PIG.

a well-known work: "The head should be set close to the shoulders to give size to the cheek, which is counted among the choicest pieces of meat. The snout should be short, the ears small and well shaped, and it is a curious fact that some of the most experienced breeders judge the general quality of the animal from the ears: if thick and heavy and much drooped they indicate coarseness; if soft and well formed, show pure breed; if sharp and upright, a restless disposition not tending to fatten quickly."

CHAPTER II.

IMPROVEMENT OF DOMESTIC PIGS.

BREEDS IN AMERICA

The pig is not supposed to be a native American, but was probably brought by the early settlers from England. Naturally enough, they were anxious to derive all possible advantages in their agricultural pursuits, and as the different breed of pigs were improved, they imported the best for breeding purposes on this side of the water. The breeders of pigs seem to have had a prejudice against the Chinese boar, imported to improve American stock, and while the pigs raised were of good quality, fair in weight when fattened, as they were not large, they were generally condemned.

BERKSHIRE

By far the best stock for breeding purposes, either in a direct and pure line or for cross, stands the Berkshire. This stock was brought into this country from England about 1832, was very favorably received, and soon became distributed in nearly every State. Through lack of good care and attention the stock began to retrograde. But this was not the fault of the pigs. They certainly could not be expected

BERKSHIRE SOW.

to thrive when they received no better care than the ordinary common stock. The owners of thorough-breds could not get a paying price for them, and the pigs came to be looked upon with disfavor by the public, the general excuse being that they were "too small." Even now farmers consider "pure Berkshire" stock very doubtfully.

SUFFOLK The success of this breed was so great that they are now probably the most generally accepted pure breed in all but the Southern States.

| IMPROVED ESSEX | The Essex never became popular in the North for no other reason than that they were black in color. They are as pure-bred pigs as can be found anywhere, and it is unfortunate that they have never gained a place on the ordinary farm.

| LARGE YORKSHIRE | The Large Yorkshire, popular in England, were imported to this country. Although importations still continue to be made of them, they have gained little place with either the breeders or farmers.

| SMALL YORKSHIRE | This pig is classed by the average farmer as "fancy stock," and has therefore never become popular. At the time it was introduced, it caused much comment among breeders, owing to its almost perfect shape. It has been exhibited under various names, according to the fancy of the owner. (See illustration on front cover.)

Of late the breeding of pigs has been practiced with more care and skill. This is especially so in the United States, where the "hog product" ranks as one of the leading agricultural exports. The breeds mentioned above are only the English stock which are best known in this country. More profit is derived from these grades as breeders than as pork producers. The farmer who sees the advantage of using the thorough-bred boar with the common sow secures the best grade of pigs. When we consider the quantity of pork to be produced, as the main item, we have in this cross what might be styled the perfect pig. The young inherit the good form, early maturity and quick-fattening propensities of the thorough-bred boar, together with the strength, appetite and digestive powers of the larger and coarser sow.

WHY IMPROVED BREEDS DEGENERATE In this day of competition, the farmer must carefully lay his foundation at the beginning, if he desires the improvements he places upon it to be permanent. It is just as easy, and vastly more profitable, to be careful in the management of the pigs as it is to be neglectful. New methods and implements are constantly being invented, and the advanced farmer works now with ease when compared with the drudgery of former days.

Refined or highly bred pigs are less able to withstand hardships, and they require more feeding and a greater amount of attention than the common pig. If pigs, and their mother before them, are furnished with an abundance of good food, the improved stock will be found to be not only superior, but much more profitable.

GENUINE THOROUGH-BRED — A frequent misunderstanding exists as to what constitutes a thorough-bred; but still with a little thought this can be explained. Pigs to be thorough-breds, must have father and mother both of one breed—both offsprings of thorough-breds. Different pure breeds united, although good blood, is not thorough-bred. Then again it is not sufficient, unless the stock is strong, healthy and able to transmit the same qualities and distinguishing traits to its young. Weak and sickly pigs, in successive litters, show that disease is in the line of descent. No matter how much the farmer may have paid for such animals, the parents may have escaped, and as it shows itself in the young, they are unfit for breeding and dangerous as food. Next to the selection of healthy stock, proper care and feeding is of the greatest importance. The pig is naturally a very clean animal, and would never sleep upon dirty straw if it could obtain clean. The pig is seen sometimes to wallow in dirty pools, but this is done to cool the skin, and it is not the animal's fault if the only water it can find is a muddy pool. Young thoroughbreds when kept in damp, dirty pens, and given inferior, scanty food, will not thrive. It will not only injure them, but the evil results will show in their young. There is no truer saying than that "like begets like," and while the tenderly reared and well-fed animals will produce strong, lively pigs, with the same certainty the neglected, ill-treated sow, will give birth to little ones like herself,—half starved and sickly. Thorough-bred stock requires a great deal of attention. If the pigs are to be subjected to neglect and uncertain management, it would be better to keep only good common pigs. If by any chance pigs have suffered from neglect, Pratts Food is invaluable, as it will assist to overcome the effects very quickly.

CARE OF THE BOAR | Abundant food is necessary to keep the young boar growing rapidly until he is at least a year old. He should be given all that he will eat; and if he gets too fat, it is better to give poorer food, instead of lessening the quantity, as it would be cruel not to give an animal all that nature demanded. In winter the boar should be fed morning and evening, boiled potatoes and coarse bran, making excellent food for him. If allowed to run about the barnyard, he will obtain much additional food to suit his taste, besides the necessary amount of exercise. In summer he will fare best if allowed to run at large in a clover pasture or be permitted to roam the fields. At eight or nine months old, if he has received suitable food and care, a well-fed thorough-bred boar will be fully grown and ready for service. From the middle of October to the first of December, when most in demand, he should be given plenty of rich food. Bran, roots and clover keep in good condition, but nothing is more necessary than regular feedings of Pratts Food. It develops him into a strong, sturdy animal, and in consequence makes him all the more valuable for breeding purposes.

THE THOROUGH-BRED SOW The sow should be treated in like manner as the boar until she is about nine months old. The farmer should exercise the same judgment in the care of his thorough-bred sow as he would over an ordinary. The milk of a sow is much richer than that of any other domestic animal, and it will tax the digestive powers to their fullest capacity to convert food into a sufficient supply to satisfy a litter of hungry, fast-growing pigs. Meanwhile the mother must sustain her own life and strength by the food she eats, and to do this the food must be liberal and nourishing. She should be kindly treated, carefully sheltered and given the regular quantity of Pratts Food daily, which will help wonderfully, whether the stock be common or pure breed ; this is the greatest help known.

PROFIT OF KEEPING THOROUGH-BREDS Does it pay to keep thorough-breds? If they are to be killed when young in order to obtain fresh pork, the answer to this question would be *no*. But if they are to be used for the purpose of improving American stock, then the answer would be quite different. The advantage derived from using the thorough-bred in this manner is admitted more and more each year. The public will accept meat only of the best quality, hence the demand for thorough-bred boars is on the increase, until now, in fact, it exceeds the supply. Farmers consent that "a thing worth doing at all is worth doing well;" therefore, the raising of pigs from best animals, in the best manner, gives the greatest profit.

CHAPTER III.

THE MOST POPULAR BREEDS IN THE UNITED STATES.

CHESHIRE OR JEFFERSON COUNTY PIG

The Cheshire pig from England, crossed with the Yorkshire, originated one of the most popular breed of pigs in the United States, known as the Jefferson County pig, or as it is called in the West, the *Cheshire*. It is large in form and famous as a profitable pork producer. The breed was first exhibited and won a prize under the name of "Cheshire and Yorkshire;" afterwards, about 1868, as "Improved Yorkshire," and has since continued to win many prizes wherever publicly shown. The finer blood of the Yorkshire has dominated, and instead of a coarse and clumsy-shaped pig, the breed is well proportioned and handsome in form. Having been kept pure and in a direct line for a long time, the same characteristics have developed, becoming fully established, and what was once a mixed breed has now become a distinct species.

CHESTER COUNTY WHITES

This breed is undoubtedly the most popular in the United States. It derives its name from the county in Pennsylvania where the breed originated. This pig is nothing more than a high grade of common stock. Its best points are that it is large and vigorous, and the sows are especially valuable to cross with a high-class or thorough-bred boar, from which can be derived a mixed breed of the best quality. They are noted for their splendid digestive

CHESTER WHITE.

powers and as rapid growers. Chester County farmers may well be proud of this breed, and it is a great source of profit to them, as thousands of this stock are shipped annually to all parts of the country.

MAGIE PIGS | From Ohio comes a pig well known to farmers and successful breeders. It is called by a number of names; sometimes "Butler County," or "Gregory Creek," after the place where it is thought to have originated, but more often "Magie," after a successful breeder. The Magie pig is a well-established breed. The best specimens of the common stock of the county are thought to have been crossed with a Poland, and their young with a Byefield. The offspring from these crosses were again crossed with the Berkshire, until, after almost a quarter of a century of judicious crossing, a breed was obtained with all the desirable qualities of a good farm hog.

POLAND CHINA.

POLAND CHINA — There are many other breeds, like the Duroc, Jerseys, Victorias, etc., that are very valuable and popular in some sections, but we have given descriptions of those of the most generally *accepted in the largest portion of the United States.* The last, but not least, to mention are the Poland Chinas.

CHAPTER IV.

PROPER BREEDING AND REARING.

PEDIGREE | The best is always the cheapest in the end. If the pigs are to be kept until fully developed, then it is important to consider the parentage. The sows of the Chester White breed make the best mothers, and they are very good to cross with. It matters not whether the boar is an Essex, Suffolk, Berkshire or Yorkshire, so long as it is full thoroughbred stock. Of course, if it is the intention to kill the pigs when small, no especial breed need be considered, so long as it is healthy and in good condition.

CARE OF THE SOW | Pigs born early in the spring can be weaned in six weeks, and the mother, if she has been well treated and liberally fed, usually breeds again the same year. The farmer or breeder should be careful, when the sow is put in the house to farrow, to begin giving her the same kind of food as she will have when suckling. At this time a strict and constant use of Pratts Food will be found to be very beneficial, both to the mother and her litter. The sow should be given a clean, dry pen, with a comfortable bed of fresh straw. Have the pen well ventilated, but no place where the wind can blow on the pigs. Do not get the erroneous idea into your head that the sow will get too fat; the better the condition of the mother, the fatter and more active will be her young. Experience shows that a sow in excellent condition is sure to have a fine litter of pigs. During this period, when she is expected to farrow, she should be given plenty of food and all the milk and slop she will drink. She will thus be better able to give an abundance of nourishing milk, and her young will thrive better, than if she was thin and half starved before their birth. All pigs need fresh water, and the sow must be given it daily, no matter how much liquid food she takes. If the farmer gives the sow this care and attention when she is about to farrow, he will have less trouble and fear of accident when she gives birth to her litter. The mother should be shown great attention while suckling. There is a great demand on her and she should be given liquid food, especially that which tends to produce rich and wholesome milk. Pratts Food can be used here with the best results. While the pigs are very young, it is wise to occasionally give the mother a cooked meal. Add the usual amount of Pratts Food to three quarts of bran; pour boiling water over it and stir constantly. After having been thoroughly scalded, allow it to stand for an hour and a half; then fill the pail with cold water and feed to the nursing mother.

THE LITTLE PIGS When only two weeks old, pigs can be taught to eat from a little trough; but if this is not fastened to the floor they will upset it in their eagerness to obtain the food.

The trough should be out of the reach of the sow, and only a quart or two of sweet milk put in it each time. At first they will waste more than they eat, but as they grow older will quickly find the bottom of the trough, which should be cleaned before the next meal is given. When a month old, they may be given a handful of oats or a little oat-meal each day. It requires great care not to overfeed them. Pratts Food should be given them from the first; it will be found a profitable investment, both in the general growth and health of the pig.

WEANING Pigs that have been taught to eat well may be weaned at six weeks, and should never be allowed to nurse more than three months. This depends upon the season of the year and strength of the mother. It is better to take the young away gradually, leaving the sick and weakly ones, if there are any, until the last. Extra attention will now have to be shown to the young, and they should be fed at least four times a day—the first thing in the morning and the last at night.

Treated in this way, they do not miss their mother and thrive just as well without her. The most suitable food for them is warm milk, and either oat or corn meal gruel. A corn-meal pudding is good, if properly stirred until all the lumps are out, and then mixed with a full measure of Pratts Food, and the pail filled up with milk. It should be carefully looked after that the young pigs are kept warm while being weaned, and for this purpose they should be put in a close-covered pen and given sufficient straw to bury themselves in. If their bedding is dry and changed often, they will cuddle together, and be as comfortable as when with their mother. To make young pigs grow and thrive, plenty of wholesome food and nice warm quarters must be provided for them. After the critical period of weaning, the management and proper care of pigs will be governed by circumstances and the surroundings, according to each farmer's best judgment.

AVERAGE WEIGHT | Pigs coming from a sow of good stock, crossed with a thorough-bred boar, and raised under the above system of feeding and care, should average four hundred pounds, dressed weight, when a year and a half old. The following table gives the weight of the different parts of a pig:

Carcass	178 lbs.,	10.0 oz.
Large intestines and contents	8 "	5.7 "
Small " " "	4 "	8.0 "
Intestinal fat	2 "	5.6 "
Heart and aorta	0 "	9.6 "
Blood	7 "	10.1 "
Lungs and windpipe	1 "	9.1 "
Stomach and contents	2 "	10.0 "
Caul fat	1 "	2.3 "
Liver	3 "	4.5 "
Gall bladder and contents	0 "	2.1 "
Bladder	0 "	2.5 "
Pancreas (sweetbread)	0 "	6.6 "
Milt or spleen	0 "	4.7 "
Tongue	1 "	0.2 "
Toes	0 "	2.9 "
Miscellaneous trimmings and other parts	0 "	15.9 "
Total offal parts	35 "	4.6 "
Loss by evaporation	1 "	2.0 "

CHAPTER V.

MANAGEMENT OF PIGS.

GOOD CARE You cannot expect to gain good results unless you adopt a liberal and humane system of feeding, especially while the pigs are young and growing. A sow that has been half starved all her life cannot produce strong, healthy pigs. Some farmers keep their breeding sows in a state of semi-starvation, thinking that to be thin in flesh improves their breeding and suckling qualities. In this they make a mistake. The sow will grow thin, while the little pigs she nurses will get fat and thrive; but this fact has nothing whatever to do with her breeding and suckling qualities.

CARE OF SOW AND PIGS After she has pigged, the sow should be generously fed upon warm slops and milk-producing food (Pratts Food is a milk producer), that she may be able to give nourishment sufficient for her family. As soon as the little pigs are weaned and begin to eat, they do credit to this advanced and better method of improving stock. Blood will tell, and the characteristics of the thorough-bred boar will show very plainly when pigs thus attended to are fully grown. Profit is on the side of the thorough-bred boar. Pigs thus parentaged will sell at two months old for a good price, while the little common pig is now seldom marketable except as food ; and at a year old the improved pigs bring much better prices than ordinary stock.

IMPROVEMENT OF STOCK

To breed pigs profitably, at least one thorough-bred boar should be kept in every farming neighborhood. A large, thrifty sow and a thorough-bred boar will produce improved stock, which, with proper feeding and care, will reach a higher standard of excellence with every generation. Each successive litter of pigs will be finer and better if the sow is liberally fed before they are born.

VALUE OF PIGS ON A FARM

Pigs are of great assistance to the farmer in turning seeming refuse into a valuable product. They are kept for different reasons, according to the owner's occupation and locality. The dairyman finds in feeding pigs the most convenient and profitable way to dispose of his skimmed milk and whey. The pig will find plenty of good food in the slops and other refuse from the kitchen, and in picking up the grain which is scattered through the fields and around the barns, and what would practically be waste.

PIGS ON THE GRAIN FARM

No matter how well fed on milk or in pasture, pigs grow faster which are given occasional rations of corn-meal, or better still corn-pudding, made by pouring boiling water over dry meal, together with the usual amount of Pratts Food, (which is one of the greatest pig growers known,) and stirring until thoroughly wet and free from lumps. A mixture of yellow corn-meal and skimmed milk forms an excellent diet, as the corn is rich in oil and starch substances.

PEAS AS FOOD FOR PIGS

Farmers, particularly in the Western States, are learning the value of peas as food for hogs. Large crops are grown every year and can be planted early on land which is to be sown with winter wheat. The peas can be fed either green or dry; but when the latter is desired, they should be soaked for twelve hours or cooked, as the farmer finds most convenient. The returns for such feeding are more solid pork and very rich manure.

RAISING PIGS NEAR A CITY

It is always a question with market gardeners, florists and seedsmen in the suburbs how to obtain a sufficient quantity of rich manure at small cost. The demand is great, and this necessarily keeps the price up. Sheep have been experimented with, but they needed clover hay, and therefore this method is known to be too expensive. The keeping of pigs meets the difficulty, and proves a most practical method of procuring rich manure at the lowest cost. The question of the best food for the most favorable results here presents itself. A table given elsewhere in this book shows the relative value of different foods in producing manure from pigs, and may be depended upon as correct.

CHAPTER VI.

VALUE OF PIG MANURE.

UPON WHAT THE VALUE OF MANURE DEPENDS

We have just been considering the value of pigs to the truck farmers and florists living in the suburbs of large cities. But others can also derive profit from this source. There seems little doubt that if well managed, this enterprise might become a paying and growing business. It would be necessary to select pigs of rapid growth, that would mature early and be ready for market when fresh pork commanded a good price. In this way pork and lard could give a profit, and the best quality of manure be obtained at less cost. Nothing is without a reason, and this seems to be the age in which the cause is given to explain the effect. The degree of richness in the manure of different domestic animals depends entirely upon the food they eat. Feed a pig and a sheep on clover, and the value of the manure will be equal. Feed one on straw and the other on clover, and the manure of the latter will be much richer. Pigs are given more nutritious food, and that containing less indigestible matter, and therefore, although less in quantity, their manure is richer in quality than that of other animals of the farm-yard.

PROFIT IN FATTENING PIGS. Counting the yield of manure in fattening pigs, no farm stock pays so well. An actual estimate is shown in the following table of the exact value of pig manure:

Value of manure in producing 100 lbs. pork from peas $3.54
" " " " " " clover 4.80
" " " " " " Indian corn . . 1.76
" " " " " " skimmed milk . 5.02
Average value from pigs fed the above four articles 3.78

With the right sort of management, the pig will not only convert food into manure, but also change other refuse into the same valuable material. A small yard attached to the pen is now considered an economy, and into this can be thrown grass clippings, weeds, vegetable tops, vines, leaves, ashes and other disfiguring rubbish about the premises. It is the nature of the pig to root, and it will turn this over and over, mixing it with manure, until it becomes a rich compost, suitable to be used in enriching the soil and containing those elements important to plant life and growth.

CHAPTER VII.

THE MODEL PEN.

LOCATION A neglected, abused pig is cross and stubborn, but among all domestic animals, not one is more easily managed, if well treated. Always keep the pen clean and dry. To wallow in dirt and filth is not considered any more a pig's proper condition. The pen should be built on ground sloping toward the barnyard, in order that the liquid, which is the most valuable part of the manure, need not be wasted. If it is not possible to secure these advantages by natural formation of the land, the high foundations should be built for the pens, with drainage into a basin or vault provided for the liquid. The straw used in bedding for pigs makes a valuable addition to the manure heap.

FLOORING — The best floor is beaten earth, because when once firm and solid it needs no repairs. The pigs, however, should be given dry, fresh earth, ashes and occasionally a little charcoal to prevent their rooting up the floor, as nature inclines them to do. Farmers say that pigs thrive better on a floor made of planks than upon a stone floor, although the latter is kept clean easier and lasts longer. The pens should be cleaned out every day.

ODOR FROM PENS — The smell of pigs kept near a house is objectionable, but with proper care this can be avoided. If the pens are at a great distance, the labor of feeding and caring for them is much increased. If the pens are conveniently built, it requires less time for the farmer to attend to his duties around them. A pig should be thoroughly washed once a week, the yard and pen scattered with dry earth, all straw used as bedding removed frequently, and a fresh supply provided. When this course is strictly followed, the smell is removed, and it must be granted that the pig gives generous return for the trouble of caring for it in the best manner. Some farmers carry on their business in all other directions with judgment, but seem to think that anything is good enough for the pigs. When kept in damp, dirty pens, wretchedly fed, and exposed to cold without comfortable shelter, they somehow manage to yield a profit; but how much greater, if well managed, liberally fed and kindly treated!

NECESSITY OF WATER Much water is needed to wash out the troughs and clean the pens, and nothing is a greater convenience than a good pump in the yard. From a trough under it, the pigs can drink as often and as much as they please. The wise farmer will remember that fresh water is a demand of animal nature, which liquid food does not supply.

PEN FOR THE BREEDING SOW Pigs born in the winter or early in the spring often die from exposure, if left in an open pen. For a breeding sow, the pen should be divided by a partition, with a sliding door, into two parts; one for eating, the other for sleeping. A warm room with a closed door affords protection for the little pigs, and makes the mother more comfortable. During extremely cold weather, a sow that has been kindly treated will permit a blanket to be put over her young, as if she understood their danger from exposure. Our illustration shows a small pen. It can be increased to any size.

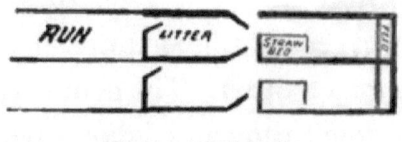

SMALL PIG PEN.

Fresh air is necessary in the sleeping apartment of the pigs, and while the sides should be boarded up tight, a single board may be hinged between the two parts of the pen. This can be opened partway to admit air, or in warm weather raised and fastened up wholly. During severe storms it can be closed, and afford perfect protection from wind or snow. These pens can be built with very little expense, are easy to keep clean, and the straw used for bedding can be quickly removed, and a new supply put in.

AN UP-TO-DATE PIGGERY In these days the well-being of animals is carefully considered. The best systems of feeding, shelter and care are generally adopted by the farmer who wishes to be successful in his business. Keeping pigs in large numbers in the same building is now considered unhealthy. They do not grow quickly or fatten readily in close and oppressive atmosphere. Many diseases to which pigs are subject are contagious, and when sheltered under one roof, if a single animal is attacked, all the herd is likely to suffer from it. The modern system of using separate pens gives no opportunity for crowding or interfering with each other. The comfort of the animals is secured, and much time and labor saved for the persons who feed and manage them. Each pen has a small yard, and the general arrangement includes the great advantage of convenience and cleanliness. It is quite as well suited for one pig, and can be enlarged to accommodate any number, without disturbing the pens already built. Each pen is separate, and yet with easy communication between them. Alterations can be made quickly at any time and with little expense. The ease with which vegetables, roots, weeds, etc., can be received, and also the convenient method of loading from each pen into the cart as it passes along a drive between the pens, are points certainly in its favor when compared with other methods.

CHAPTER VIII.

CONVENIENCES.

TROUGH — Of course the size of the trough depends on the number of pigs. The old-fashioned trough, or the original trough, is still the best for out-door feeding. It is made by hollowing out a log with an axe or adze. It is used upon a great many prosperous farms in different parts of the country.

Another simple and cheap trough is made from two-inch pine or hemlock planks. Pigs need two troughs, one for food and one for water; but if this is not convenient, the one trough can be partitioned. The log trough has the advantage of the two, as it cannot be upset.

A great many farmers think that a trough with

SWINGING DOOR TROUGH.

swinging door is the best. This door, or cover, extends the entire length of the trough, and the pigs can only eat when this is open.

Triangular pieces of wood can be placed on the door, in order to separate the pigs while eating from the trough.

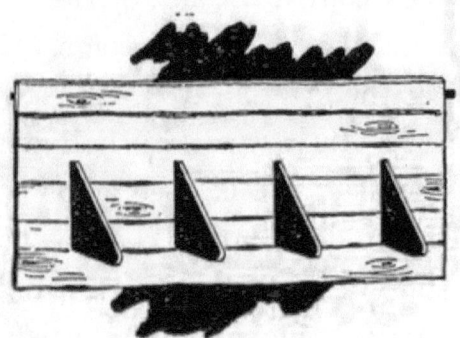

SEPARATING TROUGH.

The inventor has not forgotten the pig trough, but has presented many different styles in cast iron. They

EQUAL-SHARING TROUGH.

are sold at stores devoted to farm implements, but so far are not in general use among farmers. They vary in price and also in weight, some of them being exceedingly heavy.

There is an excellent trough which is well known to farmers; but it has one objection, and that is, it must be cleaned from the inside of the trough. The trough is built between the upright posts of the pen and projects through the boarded side. The milk and other food can be poured into it with very little trouble. If several pigs eat from it, it may be divided in sections, so that all may get an equal share.

COVERED TUB FOR GARBAGE | We have discussed to some extent the food for the pigs, and the manure and place to feed them. Now we should look and see how we should keep some of this food. The old-time swill barrel is rapidly going into decline. The tub we are about to speak of is the implement which has taken its place, and is used by a great many farmers.

It is made especially for this purpose. It is constructed of pine planks two and a half inches thick, and its size must, of course, depend upon the number of pigs kept. A convenient measurement, however, is five feet in length by two and a half feet in width, and the same in height. It has a tight-fitting cover, hinged in the middle, so that one half can be open while the other remains closed. It is not necessary to state that carrying in pails to the pig pen all the dish-water, milk and refuse from the family table is hard work. This labor

GARBAGE TUB.

is now avoided in the closely covered barrel on wheels which, when not in use, can be kept at a distance from the back door. After each meal, if necessary, it may be trundled up, filled and wheeled to the receiving tub (before described), which is kept near the pens. When emptied, it should be thoroughly rinsed with cold water. If a little corn-meal is occasionally mixed with this waste and allowed to stand a few hours before feeding, it adds much to its benefit as a diet for pigs.

CHAPTER IX.

DISEASES OF HOGS.

Before reading our suggestions in regard to diseases of hogs, read carefully the note on page 58.

PREVENTION OF DISEASES.

With the human race a patient can tell where and how he suffers, but the sickness of a dumb animal must be wholly determined and treated from symptoms. The best means to prevent sickness among hogs is to give them pure air, clean, dry pens, and plenty of good food. So many of the diseases of pigs are contagious that a sick animal should at once be removed from the herd, and put in a distant and separate pen. To prevent the spreading of disease, the troughs should be scalded, and a solution of carbolic acid sprinkled as a disinfectant about the premises as soon as the sickness appears. After this is done, dry earth must be scattered through the pens and yards. When pigs have good care, and are regularly fed on Pratts Food, there is practically no sickness among them.

HOG CHOLERA.

There has been much time spent in studying the cause of this disease. A few of the forms of hog cholera, however, may be mentioned. Hog cholera, as a rule, occurs from one of the following causes: Unwholesome food; hogs occupying one field or pen from year to year without proper cleaning or plowing the field occasionally, so as to keep it fresh and clean; hogs being constantly "rung" and preventing them from rooting in search of bugs, worms or vegetable roots; scanty feeding; muddy, stagnant and filthy water, which often compels them to drink their own urine; wet lands; decaying vegetables during dry seasons. One sick hog may affect the whole drove, and as each succeeding hog gets the disease, it seems to be a more severe case than the previous one, and becomes more and more contagious. Constant feeding of dry corn produces an inflammatory condition of the system, which invites an attack of fevers and cholera. This is the reason why sometimes apparently the most healthy and the heartiest hogs are taken with it. Then again, too scant a quantity of corn is a disadvantage. The proper feeding of the hogs should be looked after carefully, and one kind of diet should not be given in excess or in too small a quantity, either. After the disease once starts, it spreads very rapidly. An affected hog should at once be removed from the rest of the herd. Suggestions to prevent hog cholera and other disease, can be found in the paragraph heading this chapter. On account of the seriousness of this disease, we do not feel justified in giving a number of the "so-called sure cures" that have come to our notice, as we have been very careful that all which we have submitted to our readers in this work should be information of which we are certain, from actual experience of competent authorities. We know that a positive prevention of and cure for hog cholera is in the regular feeding of Pratts Food, and the following carefully of the conditions and care mentioned in our remarks in preventing disease, at the head of this chapter.

Much more could be said on the subject, but there is nothing that we could say that would add to the foregoing information and that would be of any advantage to the hog-raiser; and in writing this book, we have endeavored to give all the information we possibly could in as few words as possible. We find, as a rule, there is a great objection in requiring the reader to plod through a large amount of unnecessary matter to obtain a small amount of information, which is so common with many authors. Therefore, we have endeavored to arrange our book to obviate this objection, and have endeavored to write the book in plain, practical, common-sense form.

MALIGNANT TYPHUS FORM.

This is a form of hog cholera that will be attended by the following symptoms: **Dull, weak appearance; refusing food; unsteady walk; lying down** a great deal; rolling in the bedding; the animal shows a desire to bury its head, or even the whole body; shivering fits, succeeded by high fever; breathing quick; bowels constipated or hard, dark colored-lumps. The animal tries to vomit; in from ten to twenty-four hours the symptoms become much worse. Spots appear on the inside of the legs or on the lower part of the abdomen, and on the breast and neck. A swelling follows, **crimson** in color at first, afterwards a purple; and if the hog dies, it turns to a bluish-black color. The fever increases; the mucous membrane presents a lead-color appearance; the breathing becomes labored; the temperature, at first very high, now gradually diminishes; hind quarters become paralyzed; convulsions commence, and the animal dies in from six to twelve hours — which will be about two or three days after the commencement of the disease. If the spots are few and do **not run together,** and the fever not very great, and the other symptoms become less marked about the second day, there is a chance of recovery. Partial paralysis may remain, with loss of appetite, so that it is difficult to get the animal to eat enough. Even after recovering, care must be taken so that the digestion is not affected, and thereby prevent the hog from fattening. By making a gruel of Pratts Food and giving frequent doses, we have found it, in all cases where the proper care accompanied its use, to prove a most successful and quick-curing remedy. As per our note to give different recipes, on page 58, we submit this treatment, as follows: Give from five to twenty grains of white hellebore in a little milk. If the hog will not drink, make into a pill by mixing with flour and water. In twenty minutes the hog should vomit freely. If not, repeat the dose. After it has vomited, give the following: One-half ounce Hyposulphite of Soda; ten drops Solution Carbolic Acid; five drops Tincture of Aconite. Mix well, and add enough molasses to make a soft mass, and place well back in the throat; or, if the hog will eat, give it in milk.

Of course, the users of this treatment claim that it should be commenced early in the disease and repeated three times daily, or even every two hours. Injections of warm soap-suds into the bowels, to which half an ounce of turpentine and ten drops of carbolic acid have been added, may be made twice daily, and will help the disease considerably. The sores should be opened and bathed in warm water containing half a fluid ounce carbolic acid solution to **each pint of water.** In very severe cases we have known muriate of ammonia, in half drachm doses in a little molasses, **to be used.**

PUTRID SORE THROAT FORM.

This is a very frequent form of hog cholera that affects the throat, larynx and air passages, principally the larynx. **It at times affects the** cavity of the chest and causes congestion of the lungs. The breathing is hard and of a wheezing character. There will be a hacking cough, hoarse grunting; a great heat and dryness of the snout; swelling of the tongue; brown-red color of the mucous membrane of the mouth. Difficulty in swallowing, with attempts to vomit. The larynx and along the windpipe, even down between the forelegs, will appear a hot, hard swelling, crimson in color at first, probably changing to a lead color, and finally dark purple. The animal either tries to lie down or sits upon its haunches like a dog. Finally, the breathing becomes so **hard, he opens his mouth, the** swollen tongue will hang out. **The mouth becomes lead color.** At this stage of the disease, the hog either dies by choking or gangrene sets in.

Of course, in this form of the disease, as well as

others, we recommend **Pratts Food**, having been successful in effecting a cure in almost every instance by giving small doses frequently, making a gruel of the Pratts Food by mixed with warm water and pouring down the throat. At the same time, we mention another treatment, which is as follows (see our note in reference to giving different treatments on page 58):

Ten to twenty grains of white hellebore, to make the hog vomit; and repeat it in twenty minutes if it does not have the desired effect. Then give the following three times daily: One-half ounces Hyposulphite of Soda; one-half drachm Muriate of Ammonia. Mix with molasses to make a mass, and place on the tongue.

Five drops of tincture of aconite, dropped on the tongue in the early stages, will be of considerable assistance; and, in addition, give the following every hour, or in severe cases every half hour, in tablespoonful doses: Three ounces Chlorate of Potassa; one-half fluid ounce Solution of Carbolic Acid. One quart of water. Mix well.

As the hog gets better, lengthen the time between doses.

INFLAMMATION OF THE BOWELS FORM.

This is confined to the bowels and urinary organs, either in all at one time or separately. The bowels are costive, and streaked with mucus, and may be discolored. In the fatal stages, diarrhoea may succeed, this occurring just before the animal dies. The first symptoms are a short, hacking cough, some difficulty in breathing; unsteady walk; high fever; the animal will arch its back and paralysis will result.

For treatment of this form we recommend, as the only necessary remedy, Pratts Food in gruel form (as mentioned on another page), in case the animal is too sick to eat; if not, it can be mixed with the food, and between feeds given in gruel form. Injections of warm soap-suds, to which add half an ounce of solution of carbolic acid can be given. Another recipe, given as per our note on page 58, is calomel, as a cathartic, in doses of one scruple every six hours until the bowels are moved. Also, five drops of tincture of aconite on the tongue in early stages. After the calomel has been effective, give the following three times daily, using the aconite between the doses: One-half ounce Hyposulphite of Soda; one scruple Chlorate of Potassa. Mix with molasses to make a mass.

QUINSY.

This is termed by some as another form of hog cholera; and sometimes assumes an epidemic form similar to distemper in young horses, and is fatal to a large number of young pigs, as well as older hogs. In this fatal form it is termed hog cholera, but differs from it in not being so malignant. The symptoms are the swelling of the glands under the jaw; oppressed breathing; difficulty in swallowing. In the later stages the neck is badly swollen, the tongue protrudes and death is caused by choking. The swelling sometimes takes a gangrenous form. It is caused by exposure to sudden changes of temperature; or by bad food, impure water or filthy enclosures; and mortification at times sets in, which may cause death in a few hours. Hogs piling up around an old hayrick on cold nights will often be the cause. The ones underneath become so warm, that when routed out in the morning, the cold air striking them, the sudden change will produce inflammation of the lungs, quinsy, diphtheria, which, in a fatal form, become nothing more or less than hog cholera. Young pigs often get quinsy. They should be kept warm, clean and in well-ventilated pens; plenty of straw, and mess of gruel three times a day, in which stir the usual quantity of Pratts Food. If the bowels are constipated, Pratts Food is all that is necessary, given in gruel form if too sick to eat; otherwise, mixed with the food in large doses to move the bowels freely. It may be well at first to give in gruel form, so as to move bowels quickly. An ounce of castor oil to each pig can be added. In bad cases, to grease the throat well with equal parts of cod-liver oil and turpentine is good, no matter what remedy you use otherwise. Also, a deep cut into the tumor, from two to four inches long, and deep enough to reach the seat of the disease, will relieve it. The diet should be a thin gruel, in which a teaspoonful of turpentine can be stirred.

Another recipe given, as per our note on page 58, is: Four grains of Tartar Emetic; six grains of Ipecacuanha; six grains of White Hellebore. Mixed together for older hogs, and half this dose for young pigs.

Three or four drops of tincture of aconite, when dropped on the tongue every two hours, is said to be very excellent. However, in this disease, as in all others, we have been most successful in the use of Pratts Food alone.

DIPHTHERIA.

This happens more frequently than most people suppose, and is a contagious disease, taking an epidemic form; sometimes called a form of hog cholera. It attacks both young pigs and old hogs. It is produced by filthy pens or wet pastures. The symptoms are sudden sickness, dull appearance, loss of appetite, weakness, feverishness, stiffness of back and loins, crouching walk with head raised, mouth dry and open, hoarse grunt, livid tongue and difficult breathing. The throat is red and swollen and covered with grayish-white patches, extending to the air passages. Pieces of false membrane are coughed up. The animal lies down, or sits on its haunches, or leans against a fence while coughing, and generally dies during the coughing spells.

We state, as mentioned before, that Pratts Food, used as directed, has been most successful. Adopt the gruel form mentioned in previous diseases, and afterwards mixed with the feed. According to note, on page 58, we mention the following: Give each hog a spoonful of chlorate of potash in a small quantity of milk. Move the sick hogs to dry quarters, and give each hog daily the following: Two drachms Sulphite of Soda; one drachm powdered Castor Bean; five drops Solution of Carbolic Acid.

To those who eat, it can be given with the swill. For the others, it can be mixed with molasses and smeared on the back of the tongue. Make a small swab of sheep-skin, and swab throat out twice daily with following: One ounce Chlorate of Potassa; two fluid drachms Solution of Carbolic Acid. In one quart water, well mixed.

Flour of sulphur, sprinkled in the throat, is good. Warm, sloppy food should be given, to which may be added chlorate of potash in teaspoonful doses.

CONSTIPATION.

Do not allow the pigs at any time to become constipated. A feverish condition arises from it, developing into some inflammatory disorder. The food should be changed, from time to time, green food being the best. Many people resort to Epsom salts; but the after effect is to constipate them more than ever; the best thing known to regulate the bowels is Pratts Food, mixed with the regular feed.

SCOURS IN PIGS.

This may attack one or two out of a litter, or a whole litter when one or two days old. It seems to be an indigestion, caused by what the sow has eaten, or by the method of feeding her. Frequently, too much green clover or other green food will do it, or feeding dry corn, or musty, decayed food. While this affects the pigs, the sow is not disturbed by it. By feeding Pratts Food, this will not occur, and it rapidly improves their condition. However, as per our note on page 58, we mention the following remedy: A teaspoonful of sulphur to the sow, in a little milk twice a day. If the pigs seem to suffer too much, give twice daily, with a teaspoon, two or three drops of laudanum in sweet cream. Change the mother's food, and see that it is of good quality. Keep the pigs warm and closely penned. Do not allow them to run or exercise themselves more than can be helped. Keep pen clean and scald out trough with boiling water and lye. With proper care, the disease will disappear. If the pigs are old enough to eat, a few drops of solution of carbolic acid, added to their food will be a good thing.

CATARRH.

This develops slowly and is not noticed at first. It inflames the mucous membrane of the nose passages. It is supposed to be hereditary. The appetite fails, the animal becomes poor and has a fever. It is a disease which is not often seen; is of a scrofulous nature, often terminating in consumption. The animal should be kept dry, and given milk, boiled food, oat-meal gruel, boiled barley, mashed fruit, cabbage, etc.; food which does not require chewing is what it wants. If the bowels are constipated, first give Pratts Food in gruel form. We mention as per our note on page 58, as follows: Half an ounce of Glauber salts and a drachm of saltpetre mixed with honey, smeared well back on the tongue. Give three times daily, every other week, the following: One-half drachm of Sal-Ammoniac; eight grains of Camphor. Mix with a little molasses and smear on the tongue.

COUGH.

This is a local irritation and by many claimed again as a form of hog cholera. It is caused by an obstruction of the lungs. Pratts Food, fed first in gruel form if the animal is costive, is a sure remedy; the throat and lungs should be rubbed with a strong liniment and the animal kept well blanketed; but we mention another remedy, as per our note on page 58: Powdered castor bean, in two or three drachm doses; mixed with molasses and smeared on the back of the tongue.

INFLAMMATION OF THE LUNGS.

This is caused by sudden changes, exposure to storms, piling of hogs during cold nights. The hog will take shivering fits; is dumpish and drawn up in a heap; loses its appetite, with short breathing. The disease is generally accompanied with a cough that is deep and hoarse; also constipation.

Pratts Food should be given first in double quantity in gruel form; then reduce to the regular amount; the throat and lungs rubbed with a strong liniment. In all swine diseases the sick hogs should be separated from the rest of the herd. The diet should be warm gruel, water slops, sour milk, etc. An injection of warm soap-suds can be given. As per our note on page 58, we mention the following: A half to two drachms of saltpetre, and one to three ounces of Glauber salts, according to the size of the animal. After six hours, throw a powder of the following on the tongue three times a day: Twelve grains Tartar Emetic; twelve grains powdered Opium; one and one-half ounces Saltpetre. Mix, and divide into eight powders.

After the hog appears better and inflammation subsides, half-drachm doses of sal-ammoniac, thrice daily for a few days, will prove beneficial.

INTESTINAL WORMS.

These are noticed by the hog being unthrifty and having a big appetite. They cough, the bowels are loose, and they start from their sleep with a sharp cry and often scream before feeding-time, as if starved. Vomiting and choking fits occur from the worms getting in the throat. Pratts Food, mixed with their regular feed, will cure them. As per note on page 58, we mention: Two drachms of oil of turpentine in milk for six mornings in succession, followed by a purgative of one scruple of calomel to each hog, is said to be a good remedy; but the only treatment necessary in this, as in other diseases, is the proper administration of Pratts Food.

KIDNEY WORMS.

It sometimes produces paralysis of the hind quarters. It is seldom fatal, and generally affects more than one hog in a herd. Pratts Food, mixed with the regular feed, will prevent or cure kidney worms. Rub the loins with spirits of turpentine every other day. As per our note on page 58, we mention another remedy, as follows: A solution of arsenic in half-teaspoonful doses morning and evening, every other week for several months.

PARALYSIS OF THE HIND QUARTERS.

This is sometimes caused by worms in the kidneys. The animals show a weakness in the back, and often get up and run in a straight line quite fast, swinging to one side for a while and then go over to the other side; finally get so bad that they fall over and can only drag themselves about. The appetite is good until a few days before they die. Apply over the loins a liniment composed of one part of cantharides, two parts of olive oil and two parts of oil of turpentine. Pratts Food at first should be fed in gruel form; reduce as the animal recovers. In accordance with our note on page 58, we give the following: Three drachms of powdered castor oil seeds, and eight ounces of rye flour; mixed in a quart of sour milk or thin gruel. Give this first thing in the morning; and repeat once a week. The following may be given two or three times a day: Four grains of powdered Nux Vomica, one-half drachm of powdered Anise Seed; one-half drachm of powdered Ginger. Mix with a little molasses and smear well back on the tongue.

BLIND STAGGERS.

Generally noticed by inflamed eyes. Bowels are constipated, and pulse hard and quick. The animal runs about wildly, mostly in a circle; the breathing is labored, and the animal frequently dies in a fit of this kind. It is often caused by indigestion; feeding dry corn to young pigs when they should have a sloppy diet. Frequently, costiveness attends the other symptoms. Pratts Food should be given in gruel form in large doses, gradually reducing as the animal becomes better. Warm soap-suds can be injected in the bowels to get a quick action. Cold water should be thrown over the head, and turpentine or kerosene oil rubbed in well along the spine. Pratts Food is an invaluable remedy for blind staggers, and where pigs are fed constantly, it is never known to occur.

PROTRUSION OF BOWELS IN PIGS.

This trouble is often caused by diarrhoea and weakness. Wash the parts well with water; then apply sugar of lead and water—a drachm of the lead to a pint of water, to which add a small quantity of laudanum; then gently press the part back, pushing up the finger a short distance. Three to five drops of laudanum may be given to each suckling pig to alleviate the pain. Pratts Food, fed in the regular feed, strengthens these parts and effects a permanent cure.

PILES

Are known by blood passing off with the movement of the bowels, or blood stains around the anus. The disease is generally considered hard to cure. We would advise a change of food, such as sour milk, and especially light, digestible things for a hog in this condition. Injections of vinegar and water is good. Pratts Food, fed regularly, will cure them. Our note mentions, on page 58, we would give other endorsed recipes, so we mention : Sulphur, with **cream of** tartar, or castor oil in moderate doses. If the anus is swollen, apply vaseline or cosmoline.

RHEUMATISM.

This is shown by stiffness in the animal. Pratts Food is invaluable, but as per our note on page 58, we give the following : To move the bowels, three drachms of pulverized castor bean, to which may be added ten grains of opium, to relieve the pain ; mixed with molasses into a mass, and smeared on the back of the tongue. Then give the following : One scruple Colchicum ; one tablespoonful Bicarbonate Soda. Mix with molasses into a mass, and smear on back of tongue night and morning.

APOPLEXY.

This is practically a fat hog disease. They are dumpish, out of sorts, and drop as if shot, and appear dead, all except heavy breathing. The hog should be bled at once. Tie a cord around the foreleg above the foot ; then the artery can be seen to fill above the knee on the inside of the leg. Open it with a sharp knife, and a pint to a quart of blood should be taken. If the hog comes to, as soon as possible move the bowels by injection, and give large doses of Pratts Food in gruel form. Then feed light food for some days. Pratts Food will prevent this disease.

SCROFULA.

This is shown by weak joints in young pigs in walking. Ulcerations often appear near the joints. They frequently have diarrhoea, and the urine dribbles through the navel string. In older pigs it takes the form of consumption, and the lungs become diseased. This is a hard thing to cure. Cod-liver oil given daily and Pratts Food as a tonic is about as good a remedy as we know of.

TO PREVENT PIGS FROM EATING THEIR YOUNG.

This is very frequent in some sows, and, if prevented, they will sometimes keep their milk up, so that the pigs die of starvation. When this is not due to a diseased uterus, a mixture of ten to twenty grains of spirits of camphor, with one to three of tincture of opium, poured into the ear, will cause the sow to lie down and remain quiet for several hours, (the effect of the opium,) after which she will be rid of her feelings towards the young. Very often by rubbing the pigs with brandy, it will prevent the sow from eating them; and also put some brandy on the nose of the sow herself. The best thing, however, is to feed Pratts Food prior to the birth of the pigs, which loosens the bowels and puts them in proper shape, preventing costiveness, reducing all fever, and acts as a mild tonic.

LICE.

Apply all over the body, one part benzine, six parts soft soap and fifteen parts water; mixed thoroughly and applied with a stiff brush. Another remedy is a gallon of kerosene to five gallons water, and apply the same way. The hog pen should be thoroughly cleaned and disinfected with carbolic acid or whitewash. After the pen is once infected with these lice, it takes a long while and hard work to get rid of them. Lard oil, smeared on every hog, is good; but twenty-four hours afterward, they should be well washed with soft soap and warm water.

MANGE.

This is caused by an insect, which must be killed in order to cure the disease—not only on the pigs, but in the pens and surroundings, or wherever the pig rubs against. Coal oil is a good thing, rub well with it. Mange is shown by small red blotches or pimples, which spread. Some people give sulphur and cooling foods.

The pig should be washed with soap-suds, and, as soon as dry a good coating of the following: One quart of Whale Oil; one-half drachm of Carbolic Acid Crystals. Stir them well together, and wash off the day following.

CHAPTER X.

GENERAL REMARKS.

PREPARATION OF FOOD

Farmers have different opinions on the subject of cooked food as an advantage for fattening pigs. The best results, however, are on the side of the raw diet. Conveniences and extra labor are necessary to cook the food, and nothing is gained by it. If pigs thrive and fatten as well without it, it is not wise for the farmer to incur extra expense in adopting the cooked system. For little pigs and suckling sows, warm food in winter is a comfort; but that is all, as it does not add to the nutritiousness of food.

DISPOSITION

The pig is not naturally stubborn and obstinate, as some think. It can be led by the right man with the right method. It is quick to appreciate kindness, and, when this is used, requires neither kicking or beating to make it docile and obedient. The man who employs harsh measures soon makes the whole herd stubborn. It is remarkable to see how, if well cared for and comfortable, pigs gain habits that are quiet and desirable. At their regular time of feeding, when allowed to run in the yard, they will separate and each go to its own pen just as the cow or horse will to their stalls.

COLD WEATHER | Pigs in covered pens will eat more and grow faster in winter than those kept in the unsheltered pens of the ordinary barnyard. Pigs born in winter, unless carefully protected, often die from cold within the first twelve hours. The sow is a good mother, and the little pigs gain warmth from contact with her body; but in severe weather this is not enough. The sow and her young should be covered with a horse blanket, and if she objects, rubbing the teats gently, and speaking to her kindly, will usually make the second attempt successful. When the mother does not give sufficient milk or dies when the pigs are first born, with a little patience and effort they can be taught to nurse from a bottle. Milk warm from the cow can be given in this way, until they are able to eat from a little trough. If a sow gives a scant supply of milk, it may be increased by giving quantities of weak oatmeal gruel, in which a few scraps of meat are boiled to make it slightly greasy. Regular rations of Pratts Food will cause a large supply of rich milk, if fed both before and after the pigs are born.

FEEDING | Pigs grow faster when given milk with their food, although they must have fresh water every day as well. Feed regularly, both in time and quantity. It is not profitable to give double the amount of food that can be eaten at once, and when it is time for the next feeding, let it go by without any rations. Pigs will not thrive and fatten well, so treated, and the waste food will make the pork produced, cost much more than when gained by systematic feeding. Beets make an excellent food for pigs, and more especially sows when suckling in the early spring, before they can be put in pasture. Pigs will eat green or ripe peas greedily, and it pays to feed them whenever they can be procured as cheap as corn, because they make richer manure. Half peas and half corn many farmers think better food than either article when used alone. Bran is not of any great value for fattening pigs, unless mixed with Pratts Food in the usual amount; but in this way is fed with excellent results along with other feed. Parsnips, potatoes and turnips can be profitably raised by the farmer for winter feeding.

JEALOUSY IN THE HOG

It is claimed that all animals are jealous, and certainly the pig is not an exception, as is proved by a curious method sometimes adopted. When the farmer desires to fatten a hog quickly to extreme size and weight, as a prize winner at an exhibition or county fair, he depends upon this trait to assist in accomplishing it. At each feeding, the hog is given all it will eat; and when fully satisfied, more food is put in the trough, and a little, half-starved pig is let into the pen. The fat pig makes a glutton of itself, fearing that the poor squealing visitor will share the meal. If the little pig is to be considered, this is rather a cruel plan.

PRATTS FOOD FOR HOGS

We have endeavored to make plain the advantage of Pratts Food to hogs. The experience of feeding it for years by the most prominent pig-raisers in the United States and foreign countries, fully justify us in strongly urging a test of its qualities. If intelligently fed as instructed, the profit will be even greater than is claimed in this book. It is well to remember that it is not an experimental article, but that it has a long standing reputation of the highest possible merit.

INDEX.

PRATTS POINTERS ON COWS.

Abortion in Cows,	73
Aphtha (sore lips and tongue),	78
Ayrshire Cow, illustration of,	8
" " description of,	9
Belted or Blanketed Cow,	10
Bladder, Inflammation of,	72
Bowels, Inflammation of,	68
Breeds, choice of,	27
Breeds of Cows,	8
Breeding and Feeding,	27
Breeding, general instructions,	26
Breeding Periods,	28
Brewers' Grains,	14
Bronchitis,	64
Bull, The,	29
Butter, packing and salting,	46
Butter, preparing it for market,	45
Butter Test,	15
Butter Value of Cows,	26
Calf, raising the,	31
Calf, removing from the cow,	30
Cans and boxes for shipping milk,	54
Centrifugal Creamer, illustrated and described,	35
Choking,	71
Churning,	43
Churns,	43
Colds,	65
Colic,	70
Cooling Closet,	43
Cow Pox (Variola),	77
Cow, self-sucking,	58
Cow Shed, open, illustrated and described,	22
Cows, vices of,	57
Creameries, private and stock,	49
Creamery, modern, illustrated,	49
Cream Gauges,	14
Cream, methods of separating,	35
Dairy, An Ideal,	45
Dairy Buildings,	18
Dairy Cow, Diseases of,	61
Dairy Cow, The,	11
Dairy Cows, The Best,	51
Dairy Duties,	25
Dairy Farming, General Remarks,	5
Dairy Farm, Plan of,	6
Dairymen, What they must know,	52
Depraved Appetite,	79
Devon Cow,	10
Diarrhoea, scours,	68
Dysentery,	69
Family Cow,	21
Feeding the Cow,	28
Food for Cows,	11
Garget,	76
Grain Food,	13
Grass for Cows,	12
Herd, Forming a,	7
Holstein Cow, Description of,	9
Holstein Cow, Illustration of, See front cover.	
Hornless Cows,	11
Ice,	48
Ice Houses,	48
Impure Air, Bad effects of,	24
Jersey Bull, Illustration of, See back cover.	
Jersey Cow, Description of,	9
Kicking, How to prevent,	57
Kidneys, Inflammation of,	71
Lungs, Inflammation of,	62
Mad Staggers,	67
Milk and Cream Rules,	33
Milk, Bloody,	76
Milking Bucket,	41
Milk Cellar, illustrated and described,	37
Milk, Cooling,	53
Milking, Directions for,	25
Milk, Diseased,	55
Milk Fever,	74
Milk House,	38
Milk, How to ship,	53
Milk, Leaking of,	76
Milk Route,	53
Milk Sickness,	56
Milk, Straining the,	33
Milk Test,	15
Milk Tests, Value of,	34
Milk, Watery,	55
Packing Bucket,	47

INDEX

Pan, Dairy, ... 41
Paunch, Overloaded, ... 66
Pen, Model Calf, illustrated and
    described, ... 31
Pleura-Pneumonia, ... 77
Pleurisy, ... 63
Pratts Food, Composition of, . . . 59
Pratts Food for Cows, Value of, . 12-28
Pratts Food for curing diseases, . . 58
Pratts Food, Gruel form, ... 60
Pratts Food, How to Feed, ... 59
Profitable Cows, ... 25
Profitable Crops, ... 12
Read Carefully, ... 58
Red Water, ... 73
Rotating Shelves, ... 42
Salt, ... 16
"Schwartz" Method, ... 35
Scours in Calves, ... 70
Short Horn Cows, description of. . 8
Short Horn Cow, illustration of, . 7

Stable Cleanliness, ... 22
Stable Flooring, illustrated and
    described, ... 19
Stable for Cows, Horses and Chickens, illustrated and described, . 21
Stable, Pen and Yard, illustrated
    and described, ... 18
Stalls, illustrated and described, . 21
Stocking the Farm, ... 6
Swiss Cow, ... 10
Teats, obstructed, ... 79
Test of Foods (digestibility), . . . 14
Utensils, Dairy, ... 40
Variety of Food, ... 13
Ventilation in the Stable, ... 23
Water Cistern, illustrated and described, ... 17
Water Supply, ... 16
Womb, Inflammation of the, . . 75
Worms, ... 71

PRATTS POINTERS ON SHEEP.

Aphtha, ... 108
Bladder, Inflammation of, ... 108
Bowels, Inflammation of, ... 106
Breeds, American, ... 91
Breed, Improved Kentucky, . . . 95
Breeds, Mutton producing, ... 97
Breeds, Wool bearing, ... 96
Breeding, Care of sheep while, . . 95
Bronchitis, ... 101
Buildings, Description of, ... 86
Catarrh, ... 103
Cleanliness and Comfort, ... 97
Constipation, ... 103
Cotswold Breed, ... 94
Diarrhoea, ... 105
Dog Guards, ... 84
Ewe, Care of, ... 95
Ewes, Hurdle for, ... 96
Feed Racks, Portable, ... 88
Feeding, Regularity in, ... 90
Foot Rot, ... 107
Garget, ... 104
Grasses for sheep food, ... 83
Hurdle, Portable, ... 88
Hurdle, Stationary, ... 87
Lamb, Creep, ... 99

Lambs' Diseases, ... 111
Lambs, How to Feed, ... 98
Louse, Sheep, ... 110
Lungs, Inflammation of, ... 102
Merinos, American, ... 92
Merino Ram, See back cover.
Mutton Sheep, ... 92
Netting, for Sheep, ... 87
Pining, ... 107
Pleurisy, ... 101
Poison Laurel, ... 110
Pratts Food for Sheep Diseases, . 58
Ram, How to Choose, ... 95
Rheumatism, ... 105
Roots, Selection for Feeding, . . . 90
Scab Mite, ... 109
Shed for Sheep, ... 84
Sheds for a Few Sheep, ... 89
Sheep, Care of, ... 84
Sheep, Cross Bred, ... 91
Sheep Diseases, Pratts Food for, . 58
Sheep Farm, Choosing, ... 82
Sheep Raising, Origin of, ... 81
Sick Sheep, Pratts Food for, . . . 85
Southdown Breeds, ... 93
Tick, Sheep, ... 109

INDEX

Tuberculosis, ... 104
Water Supply, ... 83
Weaning Lambs, ... 99
Winter Foods, ... 89
Worms, ... 111

PRATTS POINTERS ON HOGS.

Apoplexy, ... 167
Berkshire Breeds, ... 119
Blind Staggers, ... 165
Boar, Care of, ... 124
Bowels, Inflammation of, ... 155
Bowels, Protrusion of, ... 166
Breeding and Rearing, ... 130
Breeds, American, ... 119
Breeds, Definition of, ... 116
Breeds, Degeneration of, ... 122
Breeding Time, ... 142
Catarrh, ... 161
Cheshire Breed, ... 127
Chester County Whites, ... 127
Cold Weather, Pigs in, ... 171
Constipation, ... 160
Cough, ... 162
Diphtheria, ... 158
Diseases, Prevention of, ... 149
Early Maturity, ... 116
Eating Their Young, How to Prevent Pigs from, ... 168
Essex, Improved, ... 121
Farm, Value of Pigs on, ... 136
Fattening Pigs, ... 139
Food, Preparing the, ... 170
Food Supply, How to Keep it, . . 147
Garbage Tub, ... 147
Grain Farm, Value of Pigs on, . . 137
Hog Cholera, ... 149
Hog Cholera, Putrid Sore Throat Form, ... 154
Hog Cholera, Pratts Food for, . . 151
Hog Cholera, Typhus Form, . . . 152
Hind Quarters, Paralysis of, . . . 164
Improving the Stock, ... 136
Jealousy in Hogs, ... 173
Lice, ... 169
Little Pigs, Care of, ... 132
Lungs, Inflammation of, ... 162
Magic Pigs, ... 128
Mange, ... 169
Model Pig, Description of, . . . 118
Model Pig Pen, ... 140
Mothers, The Best, ... 130
Odors from Pig Pen, ... 141
Peas for Pigs, ... 137
Pedigree, ... 130
Pen, Flooring for, ... 141
Pigs, Average Weight of, ... 134
Pigs, Disposition of, ... 170
Pigs, Food for, ... 172
Piggery, Up-to-Date, ... 143
Pigs, Management of, ... 135
Pig Manure, Value of, ... 138
Pigs, Natural Instincts of, ... 114
Pigs, Old English, ... 117
Pigs, Proper Care of, ... 114
Pig Raising near the City, ... 137
Pig Raising, Profitable, ... 113
Piles, ... 166
Poland China, ... 129
Pratts Food Best for Pigs, ... 173
Pratts Food, Excellent for Sow, . 131
Pratts Food for Hog Diseases, . . 58
Pratts Food for Pig Growth, . . . 137
Quinsy, ... 156
Rapid Growth, ... 115
Rheumatism, ... 167
Scours in Pigs, ... 160
Scrofula, ... 168
Sow, Care of After Birth of Pigs, . 135
Sow, General Care of, ... 130
Sow, Thoroughbred, ... 125
Suffolk Breeds, ... 120
Thoroughbreds, Genuine, ... 123
Thoroughbreds, Profit in, ... 126
Troughs, Equal Sharing, ... 146
Troughs, Feed, ... 145
Trough, Separating, ... 146
Trough, Swinging Door, ... 145
Water Supply, ... 142
Weaning Pigs, ... 132
Weight of Different Parts, ... 134
Worms, Intestinal, ... 163
Worms, Kidney, ... 164
Yorkshire, Large, ... 121
Yorkshire, Small, ... 121
Yorkshire Sow, See front cover.

www.ingramcontent.com/pod-product-compliance
Lightning Source LLC
Chambersburg PA
CBHW020259170426
43202CB00008B/440